Tales From The Dockside

J. Butler Kyle

Published by Nomad Publications NV, 2024.

First Printing, 2024

ISBN PRINT 979-8-9869686-5-0

Nomad Publications NV, Wellington, NV 89444

nomadpublicationsnv@yahoo.com

Cover art designed by Heidi Thompson, Bristlecone Studios

Table of Contents

Dedication

Husband, this book wouldn't have been possible without you.
Thanks for being the reason it was written! Love you very big!
To Rusty Butler, in memory.
You were the most kind and generous badass
I ever had the privilege to know. Miss you my handsome nephew.

Acknowledgements

Writing has always been a cathartic exercise for me. But keeping a journal of our travels and adventures was just something I did. That is until people were asking questions about what it was like to live on a boat. I realized I could turn the journal excerpts into a story. Thanks to all these people, including the many colorful characters that lived on the docks with us.

It's my beta readers that keep me on my toes, and it's because of their efforts that the story reads as well as it does. Thank you so much for your time, your questions and input, and for being my friend.

Many thanks Judy Gianarelli, you were my first friend on the docks and those cups of tea were ever so special, miss you girl!

Lauren Saunders and Debbie Lemmer, dragging those little details out brought back so many memories, thank you!

Jack Butler, you are a doll for being my champion, and nagging me to finally get this done! Love you my brother!

To a very special woman in my life, Evanna Judkins, I can never say enough how much you mean to me. Your encouragement and faith in me fills my heart. Thank you is so small for how big it needs to be.

Prologue

For nearly twenty-five years we lived in an RV and traveled around the country because of Bill's employment. In 1993, we took our motorhome to Alaska where the job was for the better part of nine months. Finding an RV space proved to be impossible. We were happy to pay $250 to park in the driveway of a heavy equipment construction yard. When we were sent to a float camp for over three weeks, leaving the kitties and motorhome behind, in the care of a complete stranger, we decided a boat would be the only way to return to Alaska. Thus began the adventures of living on the water in a 28' Bayliner in the Gulf of Alaska.

We hope you'll enjoy this slight snippet into our world.

Bill & Jan Kyle

Looking for a Boat

Tuesday - January 4, 1994; Port Orford, Oregon
-—The project manager, Bart, called and said we had to be in Craig, Alaska by March 15. We drove into Coos Bay, about an hour up the road, and bought a Boat Trader magazine. We found a 30' 1955 Bryant and plan to go to Seattle next week to look at it. -—*(excerpt from Jan's journal)*

Wednesday - January 5; Port Orford, Oregon
-—Driving through Bandon, we went past the docks and saw a houseboat. On further inquiry, it was 50'x15' and only $12,500! Bad News, no engines. We've never lived on anything so big! Guess we won't now, either.—- *(excerpt from Jan's journal)*

Sunday - January 9; Port Orford, Oregon
Slowly we left the RV, headed for Brooks. The sun was dazzling the waves on the ocean. We made a leisurely stop in Coos Bay to visit with family, then on our way by 3 PM. About an hour before we left, I'd given Moldie half a kitty downer and she was fairly relaxed. By the time we got on the road again, her poor little eyes were crossed.

Passing the elk viewing area east of Reedsport, we saw two different groups. The bull elks were standing in one group and yearlings in another. They are *so* big and beautiful to watch.

The weather wasn't too bad. Near 5 PM we stopped in Drain at a hamburger joint for dinner. Fog was beginning to form near Curtain, but by Eugene, it had dissipated and begun clearing. We took a quick stop at Irwin's Boat Center in Eugene, where we learned the name of a little houseboat that intrigued us, a Yukon Delta. Somewhere around 7 PM we pulled into the Cottage, what we call the house at Brooks, Oregon.

We are here for a week to find a boat and a van, see the doctor and dentist, and fix all the little things that didn't get done over Christmas.

Monday - January 10; Brooks, Oregon

The day dawned bright and sunny with promise. The temperature was fairly high in the 50s or low 60s. Our first stop was to see Landon, a friend and owner of a Marina. He tried to talk us into buying a sailboat. To prove his point, he walked us down the dock to a 10'x30' Catalina. He said they were the roomiest boat in the industry.

It was like our live-aboard friends' boat. You climb down a four-step ladder and your face is near eye level with the water line. True to Landon's word, the boat was wide, but it felt dark and enclosing. There were a few oddities that could be called fun, but not enough to make it livable.

The next boat Bill wanted me to walk on was a 25' Bayliner. After climbing on board, again descending two steps, we found the interior had gotten wet and was damp and moldy smelling. It only took a few seconds for me to decide that I didn't like this boat at all.

Already this project was turning out to be trying.

A bit later one of Landon's employees pulled the Bayliner out of the hangar and parked it alongside the dock. Knowing I was going to have to get used to this sooner or later, I once again went aboard the Bayliner. This time it was light and seemed almost airy. I thought I could live in that space.

Maybe.

We finally left Landon and drove to Hayden Island. The Hayden Island Yacht Center was the first one we came to. Once inside, the salesman asked if he could help us. Bill didn't hesitate to let him know we were only kicking tires, but wanted a 30' boat to live on and had little money. The fellow looked thoughtful and then pointed out to a side lot where a huge boat sat by itself. He said it was the only boat he had that was in our price range and size.

Running out in the rain, he unlocked the gate. Immediately his phone began to ring, so hurriedly he told us to look at our leisure, then ran back inside.

We climbed on the boat and under the canvas, opened the door, and stepped down into the room. It was obviously a 1970s model because of the glaring orange plaid seat cushions. The room was small, but no smaller than the second motorhome. Storage was limited, but not much worse than the current motorhome. We looked at each other with that excited-worried look and climbed down.

It was sitting on a trailer, but Bill said for $12,500 that couldn't be part of the deal. Looking back up at the boat, we could tell that the two sets of canvas covering the back deck and upper deck were almost new.

Before we had a chance to talk, the salesman was back. As it was almost 3 PM, we asked if he was going to the Boat Show that afternoon. He said yes and it would be warmer and dryer there, and then we could talk, but oh by the way, was the boat something we might be interested in? We told him yes, but that we were going to Seattle on Wednesday to look at another one, but would get back to him soon.

I told him seeing this one made me nervous because Bill and I are notorious for buying the first thing we look at. Bill asked if the trailer was included and much to our surprise it was. We looked knowingly at each other, thanked him for his time, and left.

Leaving there, we drove on out Hayden Island to the other marinas but didn't find anything. Then we went back over the bridge to Pier 99. The salesman did nothing for me. His attitude was he didn't care if we bought a boat from him or not. But he did take the time to show us three different boats.

The first one was a beautiful little thing that had belonged to a Grandma and Grandpa. Although the price was good, it was so pretty and well-polished that we didn't feel comfortable taking it to Alaska where it could become trash in the unknown elements.

The second one was only $7995, but he felt sure we could take it home for $6995. It was a 34' Fairliner, and though it was definitely livable, it also had a definite case of dry rot.

The third boat was the same as a friend's boat in Alaska, a Bayliner already parked in the harbor at Craig. We weren't able to see the inside floor plan of this particular one, but it didn't really matter because although it had two engines, only one of them worked. We took all the spec sheets, thanked the fellow, and left. Getting in the car, we both agreed that the one at the Yacht Center was very much in the lead.

By this time it was after 3 PM, so we could go to the Boat Show. Because of the rain and weekday afternoon, there weren't very many people there. This was nice as we could wander around without worming our way through throngs.

The boats on display were of course decked out. Bill went on board a 4788. That's a boat about 50' long and has two to three floors and sells for about

$450,000-plus dollars! As I knew it couldn't compare to what we were going to buy, I had no desire to go in it.

We came across the salesman from the Yacht Center and he suggested we fill out a pre-credit application so he could take it over to the bank booths in time for us to know something by the next morning.

Leaving him, we wandered around. One of the displays that caught our eye was a vacuum food sealer. Of course the salesman did a splendid job showing it and we bought one. Yet, if we can get it to do half the things he did, it will work out well.

One demonstration he showed us was sealing a bulky sweater, pants, and a pair of socks in a baggie. When sealed, the whole package wasn't any larger than a big dictionary.

The most fun item he sealed was a jar of miniature marshmallows. At first, they looked like hard little mints, rather than marshmallows. This made sense in a few seconds. As he sucked out all the air, they started to grow and even float. When he was done, he made a few comments and then showed how to unseal the jar. As he popped the top off, the marshmallows UN-exploded and crumpled into little heaps of nothing! How funny!

We figure if nothing else it would seal any halibut or salmon we might catch, making them easier to ship. Soon we went home, heads spinning with information on Smoker crafts, portable hangars, boating insurance, and conversation with other used boat booths.

Tuesday - January 11; Brooks, Oregon

This was not a day for dealing with boats. Although Bill called the Yacht Center twice to see if the loan was approved, neither time was the salesman in. Of course just a few minutes after Bill and Dad left, the fellow called back. The bank had okayed the loan, the boat was going to be ours if it was sound... and if we wanted it (did we??).

That morning I had a Dentist appointment and Doctor in the afternoon. Dad wanted Bill to go with him to the auction, so we kissed and went our different ways.

When I finally pulled in well after 4 PM, I could see Bill out in the back pasture unloading junk from a white van onto the burn pile. Hoping he was unloading stuff for an unknown friend; I was reluctant to find out if we owned this massive ugly whiteness.

When I got close enough to look at it, it was awful! Bill said he had spent two hours ripping sheetrock and insulation out of it, so this looked good! But hey, for $400, what did I want?

Wednesday - January 12; Brooks, Oregon

We were up and out by 8 AM. Dad came along with us to give us his opinion if the Bayliner was worth buying. We stopped by Ryan's Marina first to see if our friend who owned the marina could come along too.

Landon wanted a description of the boat, but when Bill told him what engines were on it, he pulled an awful face, groaned, shook his head, and said we definitely did NOT want this boat.

Fearing just this sort of thing, I knew I didn't want to have to look any further for a boat. But Landon agreed to ride over with us, to help us save face.

The weather was gray and drizzly. When we got to Hayden Island no one was around, so Bill and Landon went on the boat to look things over. All the way there Landon had told us nightmares of OMC engines, the cost, the unreliability, and more. When we walked up to the boat, I was dreading Landon's reaction. I hadn't realized how much this particular boat meant. Not that *it* was so wonderful, but in very little time we had accomplished the looking part.

Landon glanced at the trailer and said it would do. He then ran his hand over the frame (or *hull*, as true terminology was slow in coming), then rounded the corner to the engines.

Without knowing I'd been holding my breath, I found I was waiting for the exclamation to come, but was shocked when Bill looked back at me and gave the thumbs up. I couldn't believe it, Landon had changed his mind, now these engines were ok? I ran up to Bill and said what does this mean? He smiled and said the engines weren't OMC after all, they were Volvos! Boy were we delighted.

So far so good.

After our friend crawled over the boat more, he got a hammer and started pounding on the back (or *transom*). Even I heard the difference in the tone of the ring. One second the thud was solid and firm, the next squishy and dull. Ah ha! This would be the downfall.

Sure enough, Landon asked if I could hear the difference. I said yes and he said that was dry rot. How could there be dry rot in a fiberglass boat? Turns out the ribs (or *stringers*) are made of wood.

Landon tapped a bit more and then said it was time to bring out the salesman. He said that little bit of thud should be worth about $1,000 off our total bill. $1,000!! Then it must be pretty bad I thought. Bill and Landon talked it over, then I went for the salesman.

He was surprised to see me as he hadn't noticed us drive in. I told him Bill was already listening to the engines run. He came out, but hesitated when he saw Landon. He had told us to bring someone to check the boat, but I don't think he expected us to get a marina owner/mechanic.

I climbed back into the cabin. Bill was on the ground by the engines. Landon was upended with his head down in the engine well, tapping on the wood and carrying on about the dry rot. With only a little theatrics, I asked the salesman what would happen if the insurance company wanted this surveyed and there was all this DRY ROT.

The fellow said it wasn't really a problem, but I wasn't convinced. Dry rot, means <u>rot</u>, rot means *unstable*, unstable means we **sink** right in the boat basin! He said it wasn't all that difficult to fix, all we needed to do was take a piece of plywood and glue it over the rot. I couldn't imagine doing such sloppy work and asked him if that fixed the problem or gave it more to feed on!

By the time I asked all my usual questions, the salesman was flustered, and Landon kept his head down so the guy wouldn't see him laughing. Nervously, the salesman told us to check out anything we wanted and to let him know when we were ready to deal, then hurried back inside. Poor fellow.

In the meantime, Dad had quietly been taking all this in, just standing back. We all got off the boat and stood inside the hangar out of the rain to discuss our findings. Landon asked what the original price was, Bill told him $12,500, but they'd dropped it to $11,500 for us. Landon said we needed to negotiate another $1,000 off if they'd do it. He said for $11,500 it was a good deal, but $10,500 would be better.

Now neither Bill nor I like to haggle, so squirming, we asked if it wasn't okay to stay at the $11,500 if we were happy with that? Dad piped up and said we should try to get the extra $1,000 off. Reluctantly we said okay. Landon asked if we'd run him back to his shop before we started the paperwork. I ran to tell the salesman what was happening.

As I walked in the door, he asked if we were ready. I told him we had to take Landon back to work, but we'd be right back. Then with a deep breath I took the plunge and asked if the fellow was firm at $11,500, and what about radios, etc. The fellow turned to me, and gave me what felt like a piercing stare, then said there were radios, and what did we feel we should pay. Then he amended himself and asked what our 'Coach' had told us.

Diving right in and thanking God later for having a quick tongue, I told him quite frankly Landon had said the $11,500 was a really good price, (*pause*) for *Here*. But to go to Alaska with known problems, the price wasn't good because we wouldn't be able to fix it as easy and even perhaps as adequately as (*emphasis*) *Here*.

The salesman agreed and asked what we thought was a fair deal. When I hesitated he said go back to our 'Coach', talk it over with him and when we got back we could work it out. I said fair enough, and rushed outside breathing once again.

When I got back to the fellows they wanted to know what the guy had said, so I repeated the whole story, perhaps embellishing on my boldness just a bit.

After returning Landon, it was time to haggle. The salesman asked aloud what price we thought was good. When Bill didn't speak up, reluctantly I asked if $10,000 was okay. Webb said how about $10,500, we said fine, consider it done.

Negotiating is so hard.

While signing the paperwork, I called my sister Jean to let her know we were ready for their truck, and she would drive up to meet us and ride back. The evening before we'd made arrangements to call before noon using a special signal of rings because she didn't want to work that day. Remembering to do this, I was surprised by the second round and second ring, she hadn't answered.

Thinking I'd dialed the wrong number, I let it ring a few more times then dialed again. Three rings, hang up, five, six, seven rings, still no answer. Figuring she must have taken the dog out for a quick walk; I told the salesman I'd try back in a few minutes.

By now it was going on 11:30 AM. Bill and Dad had gone out to take the canvas down from the deck, make sure the top canvas' were secure, and load up the spare tires. After a few minutes I tried again, and again, until nearly noon. We decided to grab a quick lunch and then try yet again.

We drove up to Waddles for lunch. Having heard lots about it on the radio, we were disappointed when it turned out to be nothing more than a spiffy truck stop, popular with the businessmen.

Twice more I called Jean, unbeknownst to me, she'd forgotten we were going to use her truck. Quickly, I called my brother, Jack, and explained the situation. He said to come get his truck at work. I agreed and we headed out, south on I-5.

As you can guess, what should have been a simple process of bringing the boat home, wasn't.

As soon as Bill hooked up the boat to Jack's truck, we headed off Hayden Island southbound. Dad and I ran traffic interference behind him in the jeep.

Hayden Island is the last piece of land before crossing the Columbia River north into Washington. The way the road is, it almost makes a cloverleaf. To start off, Bill was in the wrong lane. I could have blocked him but he didn't co-operate. All I'll say is we circled the island *twice* before we finally got back southbound on I-5 going in the right direction.

A few miles south on I-5, we took the exit to cross east on Marine Drive, so we could take the lesser traveled I-205 southbound. Once again, my nearsighted-navigator was in the wrong lane and immediately we were northbound on I-5, headed *back north again* for Hayden Island.

This time Bill knew the drill. Quickly we cloverleafed and were southbound on I-5 again. Knowing which lane would be needed, Bill was ready and with no further mishaps we continued east on Marine Drive.

(Confused yet? Just wait!)

Now the last time we had driven this area near Portland International Airport, when one leaves Marine Drive to get to I-205, they must turn south on a short block. Then turn back west on Airport Road, but be in the left lane and zoom up the I-205 ramp southbound. Turn your back and they change everything.

While I blocked traffic for Bill to get in the left lane, too late I noticed the ramp now went right and swung back round south!

Fortunately there were few cars so Bill drove past the on-ramp and pulled over. I jumped out and ran up to see what was wrong when he had the hood up.

I asked what was it? He yelled at me something about the oil pressure. Knowing there was oil in the back seat, I asked if he wanted me to get some. He yelled back NO! I yelled in return *FINE!* Then started stomping back to the jeep. Bill broke the anger when he asked if I liked the scenic tour of Hayden Island. We both laughed and the tension was eased. Apparently Jack's truck wouldn't, or couldn't, get over 40 mph and was screaming full speed in second gear.

Maneuvering our way out of airport traffic, we were able to get up on I-205 southbound without further delay. By now it was rapidly approaching 4 PM and the early stages of Portland rush hour traffic. Although we were on the freeway, Bill was running in the right-hand emergency lane. I kept behind him of course, with hazard lights flashing.

As we approached the I-84 off ramp, Bill suddenly darted left across it into traffic and continued on his way. I wasn't able to move over as a semi had me penned in, and abruptly Dad and I were now *eastbound* on I-84!

Almost as if wondering aloud, Dad sounded puzzled when he asked if we were now going south on I-5. Glancing at him incredulously, I shouted back in frustration, *NO! NOW we were headed east for Idaho via I-84!!*

It was thirty miles later before we were able to find a returning westbound off ramp, thanks to construction. All the while I was thinking colorful thoughts of my dear husband.

By the time we were headed back south on I-205, traffic had built up and all lanes were stacked. Nearing the huge Clackamas Town Center mall, traffic came to a halt because of an obvious accident. While I couldn't see the actual wreck, I could see several cops, fire trucks, and ambulances. As we inched our way I prayed it wasn't Bill, but feared the worst. Somehow Bill had been in an accident and the boat had burned to the ground. By the time we edged abreast, I was so relieved that it wasn't him I nearly cried.

By 7 PM, when Dad and I finally got to Brooks, I was horrified to find Bill wasn't there even though he had been ahead of us! The truck didn't have brakes or lights and was doing 15 mph on the freeway last I saw him. Obviously this must mean he was in trouble somewhere.

Jack and I jumped back in the jeep and went looking for him. Quickly we cruised back to the last exit I had seen him, craning our necks to look down off-ramps and visible side streets. By 9 PM we had only worked our way halfway down the twenty mile long I-205.

Quite frightened but needing fuel, we pulled into a gas station. Jack called home to let everyone know where we were and see if anyone had heard from Bill.

Need I say he had pulled in within five minutes of our leaving?

After we got separated, he had had to pull off the freeway because it was getting dark. Using all back roads, we had missed him somewhere between Aurora and Woodburn, less than five miles apart.

Though by no means was his trip as traumatic as ours, it was nonetheless harrowing. As soon as he drove in the driveway and parked the boat, he climbed up on the deck and threw the anchor overboard, proclaiming, "It's here!"

Grateful but exhausted, the boat was delivered to its first destination.

We spent the next several weeks arguing over a name. I wanted something to do with migrant or nomad (this was no-mad whim!) or maybe flotsam (float some, get it??). Bill wasn't the least co-operative. In the end, or perhaps was it in the beginning, he had decided on calling it *M/V ROTORWASH*. (M/V is for Motor Vessel.)

The original name was *HI-LILY HI-GENE*, definitely not our style. When we told our live-aboard sailboat friends we had renamed it, the woman became very excited, exclaiming we shouldn't have done that without making amends, worried about boating superstition and such. Nervous enough already, I asked what could we do to make it right? She said in renaming a sailboat one would secure a silver dollar face up to the main mast, right in the center. She assumed it would be the same on a regular boat.

When we were able to get in *ROTORWASH* we did the ceremony. Unfortunately, we didn't have a silver dollar nor did we have a main mast. But we figured a Canadian "Loonie" dollar would do, with the picture of a loon on one side and Queen Elizabeth on the other. So with the gold loon face up and centered over the doorway on the dash, we taped it secure and again named her, *M/V ROTORWASH*.

Within a month we had moved to Elkton, Oregon, and spring-like weather arrived. As Bill's employer couldn't decide when we would be leaving for Alaska, we brought the boat down, uneventfully I might add, so as to be able to work on it. When Bill tore into it, he found it needed lots of work, there was no water heater, there was only an electric refrigerator, and the stove ran on alcohol.

Of course Bill wanted to make sure the engines were in top running order. And immediately we knew the bright orange and yellow plaid cushions and same vibrant color nautical chart curtains had to go. (We replaced them with a calming morning glory panel over a mauve background and off-white curtains with a little lace trim).

While in Brooks, Jean and I had gone shopping for 'disposable' things on the boat, in case it didn't float. Besides a new wardrobe for me (Goodwill, five outfits under $20! After all, what if my other favorite clothes molded or something!), we also got some cheap pots, pans, and a cute set of wood-handled silverware that actually float! Then we found these "water socks." They are a nylon-mesh rubber-soled shoe. We'd never seen anything like them, so we bought two pairs each,

A lovely day occurred and Bill decided it was time for the maiden voyage. Calling his brother in Coos Bay, we told him we were on our way and he agreed to meet us at Ten Mile Lake. He's had a boat for decades and is quite experienced.

Leaving the RV park was nerve "wrecking," but we did okay. Once on the highway though we couldn't seem to build any speed, but were steady. Within ten miles of the RV park, the truck said no more and quit. Explicitly, Bill voiced his opinion and we were able to limp back to the Elkton, a simple clogged fuel filter causing the problem.

The next lovely weekend turned out much better. Stopping in Reedsport, we bought some plastic wine glasses and a bottle of non-champagne. Meeting Bill's brother at the lake, the first challenge was getting the boat off the trailer. As novices, we learned several do's and many more don'ts.

Discovering I was a worthless deckhand, I became quite the passenger. Bill and his brother sat on the upper deck, (or *flying bridge*) steering from there. With my feet propped up on the rail, I lounged on one of the cushions watching the maneuverings.

Steering us in little circles and then larger sweeping ones, both Bill and his brother turned, watching expectantly right. Imagine their looks of surprise when the boat turned abruptly left. An engine had died.

Then one time, Bill was in the cabin below steering and his brother was above. Wanting to see what Bill was doing, his brother started down. They met at the ladder. Each exclaimed who's steering!, and ran to their respective

13

helms! I had wondered why we seemed to be wandering haphazardly through the water.

Finally, we motored for the Coos Bay Yacht Club. A bit more maneuvering both back and forth, high speed and not, then we were neatly alongside the dock. Before I had a chance to get the mock-wine, Bill's brother pulled out the real stuff. Sprinkling droplets around the decks and over the engines, he christened the boat "seaworthy." After a sumptuous repast of smoked salmon, cheese, and crackers, the fellows decided it was time to head back and see what it would take to get the boat *out* of the water.

Lining up perfect on the ramp, Bill hit the throttle and slid up on the trailer only to miss the bow line. Time and again he tried, then finally settled in. What a sigh of relief to see the truck grunt up the hill and top over the ramp onto level ground. (It would be some time before the boat was weighed, but when it was, the grunting truck was expected at 10,500 pounds, *empty*!) The return trip to Elkton was pleasantly blasé.

Northbound

It wasn't long after this we packed up and moved north. Bill drove the boat up to Seattle and stuck it on the barge with the rest of the Company's equipment. Being a scaredy-cat, I let him and Dad go it alone. Leading the convoy, according to Bill, the trip was rather uneventful, although the 'direct route' into the shipyard, was actually 'scenic', if you know what I mean!

The first year Bill went to Prince of Wales, it was only the crew. No wives or family. Bill didn't want to go back. So he told his boss he wouldn't unless I was able to go with him. They wanted him up there badly enough they not only let me go, but everyone else's family. That first trip was a logistical nightmare for the ferry workers. It took a couple hours trying to puzzle-piece together the eight or nine 30'-35' motorhomes and travel trailers.

Thursday - April 7; Brooks, Oregon - Anacortes, Washington

-—We *finally* got on our way 3:30 PM! Poor Keaton, another mechanic and friend who rode up with us, must have thought we left him. Rather than excitement, it was mild relief to be leaving, and tension for the push to come. The weather was terrible with driving rain. We spent ten minutes at friends in Lilliwaup, then raced to Port Townsend. We sat in the ferry line less than half an hour and then crossed to Whidbey Island. We arrived in Oak Harbor about 10 PM, but nothing was open for dinner. At 10:45 PM we were eating pizza in Anacortes. We slept in the van in the ferry line, as we leave at 7 AM. -—*(excerpt from Jan's journal.)*

Friday - April 8; Anacortes; Washington - Merrill, Vancouver Island, British Columbia

-—The morning started with a bang, literally! When the ferry man *banged* on the side of the van to wake us all up! 4 AM no less! We weren't the only ones sleeping in line.

The ferry ride through the San Juan's was dark and drizzly, which gave the islands a quiet beauty. Keaton walked around outside and saw some goats. Bill and I stayed inside and saw an eagle.

Arriving in Sydney, British Columbia, we had to clear customs. They asked if we'd ever been convicted of a DUI, Bill and I both said no, looked at Keaton and he said no too. We both looked away but it was too late. They sent us into Immigration. This time they even took us inside a little room (at least they didn't close the door!).

Vaguely I worried if this would be like the movie *"Midnight Express"*, and they'd close the door and we'd never be seen again.

The Immigration fellow was pleasant, took our drivers' license, and asked why we were sent to him. We all looked innocent, unknowing. He left to confer, came back and asked again if we'd been convicted. I looked down shaking my head no, Keaton said no, and Bill stuttered. The fellow knew we were lying and asked Bill why he felt guilty. Bill finally said it must be because he's a Crew Chief and is always bailing his guys out of jail. Lame excuse.

They confiscated the pepper spray and sent us on our way. We got in the van and exclaimed at Keaton. He said if he'd told them he had been arrested (but not convicted), we'd probably never left customs. Come to find out, if he'd told the truth they would have sent him back to the U.S.!

With a driving down pour and dampened spirits, welcome to Canada.

When we first planned our trip north, traveling by ferry all the way, we had planned several stops along Vancouver Island. This included refreshments at a tea house, spirits at a pub, of course Bucchart Gardens, and an aviation museum. Wrinkling our noses at the weather, we were in no hurry to get out of the van.

Despite the slow drizzle, we stopped at Bucchart Gardens anyway. It was lovely. They gave each of us an umbrella and a map. It was too early in the spring for much to be in bloom but it was obvious even now how magnificent the gardens could be. My favorites were the rock quarry and Japanese garden. It was actually a blessing the weather was bad as we'd have probably missed our ferry otherwise.

We knew the island was near two-hundred eighty miles long. Easy right? WRONG! What we didn't know was the first one-hundred fifty miles was done at thirty miles per hour and a red light about every five blocks! Compare it to going up your local business route at quitting time! However, when the city limits *stopped,* it <u>stopped</u>! The remaining one hundred miles was a breeze through uninhabited country and virtually no traffic.

When the fan belt broke on the van, we were lucky to find a crummy little RV park at Merrill, BC, to spend the night while the boys fixed it. Essentially Bill and I are ignoring each other, too much tension from the move I suppose. Riding in the van as a passenger isn't fun either, you can't see anything from the couch through the side window and I don't feel right making Keaton sit in the back. -—*(excerpt from Jan's journal.)*

Saturday - April 9 Merrill; British Columbia -waters outside Prince Rupert, British Columbia

-—This last portion of the drive was a breeze. The weather was almost nice. We got into Port Hardy an hour before our ferry was to depart. Unfortunately, we discovered they only allow two propane tanks per rig! Bill found a flatbed to take our others. The ferry wasn't as big as we were used to, but the prices hadn't changed! Coffee and tea, $1.50!!

When night fell, I was really tired. Keaton had disappeared hours earlier. Later we found he was in the solarium. I went to one of the rear lounges and crawled in under a row of seats to avoid being stepped on. The floor was hard, but at least I could stretch out. Despite our peevishness toward each other, I awoke during the night to find Bill sleeping vigil over me in the chairs above.

The rest of the trip was unremarkable, so much so, a month later I couldn't even remember any details. -—*(excerpt from Jan's journal.)*

Life on "Island Time"

"Excerpts from a Letter"

June 13; Craig, Alaska on the Island of Prince of Wales

We got here the first part of April, after months of hassles from the Shop. It felt so much like coming home. The Northern Lights even welcomed us that first night. We love it here and wish there were some way we could stay. Unfortunately, with the world timber market so shaky, we aren't even sure we'll be back next year.

Last year we came up with our motorhome, the Enterprize. With no RV spaces available, this year we decided that a boat was much more practical. So we got *M/V ROTORWASH*, a 28' Bayliner.

Life on *ROTORWASH* isn't like being in the Enterprize (Our name for the 30' Revcon motorhome we usually call home). Our living space is about 10' long (three short paces for me) and 2' wide in the walkway. When we first arrived, we were a bit testy with each other. Good luck trying to pass your partner in such cozy quarters without touching!

Before we left the Lower 48, Bill had converted the stove to propane after he lit the alcohol stove and had to frantically fan the flames away from the overhead cabinet. Besides he said, it smelled bad. The cabinets are big enough to hold the four-each all-plastic plates, bowls, and two glasses. Silverware, (wood handled that should float) and cook utensils went in a fat, plastic jar at the back of the tiny plate-sized counter space between the single sink and stove. Also up there were some canned goods that we store upside down. (Having lived in an RV long enough in humid environs, I knew that when the cans rust, at least when you turn them back right-side up, it will be clean and free of rust.)

There was one fair-size cabinet under the sink that the two thin-aluminum pots, plastic mixing bowl, cookie sheet, small aluminum bake pan, as well as dish soap and few cleaning supplies we kept, all lived. Plus the bin of cat food and some cans for them.

One of the dinette bench seats held the water tank. The other was where we could keep our winter gear, some of Bill's tools, boxed goods and a few more canned, the kitty litter, as well as a second set of sheets sucked down in a Ziplock.

The bedroom is called a V-Berth. That is an accurate description of the shape, a V-wedged cabinet. We slept at a diagonal across the way so Bill can fit without curling. Dimensions might be a six-foot triangle, all cushions, no walking, standing, or sitting, as the ceiling is less than two feet from ones face. Our two sleeping bags are zipped together and I sewed two flat sheets together for the inside. That helps keep them from becoming too much of a tangled mess. (Does the word claustrophobia come to mind? And dare I add that the *five* of us sleep like sardines? That is Bill, the three kitties Sweetpea (30 lbs), Stinkpot (10 lbs), Moldie (15 lbs), and myself! But I must say, at night, the water lapping against the hull is rather soothing.—-

There's a diagram of the boat at the back of the book.

-—April 17 - "Didn't sleep well, sure hope we get used to that 'hole'!" -—*(excerpt from Jan's journal)*

It has taken awhile to learn some of the little idiosyncrasies. Such as turn on the water pump before you try to turn on the water faucet. Make sure after the water pump is on while taking a shower, that you turn on the overboard pump to empty the shower. Don't use too much water, otherwise the tanks need filling every day. Etc. We both laughed and thought about what life might be like when we get back in the Enterprize.

The closet is eight inches wide. Can you imagine how luxurious the four-footer is going to be?! The down side for Bill, now that we have done so nicely with so little, I want to take up some of that four-foot closet and get a mini washing machine. Bill and I have yet to see eye-to-eye on that one, but he'll come round soon, I'm sure.

Launching of *M/V ROTORWASH*

-—April 20 - "The Harbor Master came by and told us our slip is ready. As soon as we get a water heater element we'll be ready to move in. Imagine *hot water*!" -—*(excerpt from Jan's journal)*

-—April 24 - "We had to wait for high tide at 1 PM because 6:30 AM was a minus tide. Charlie and Jasper, both friends and pilots, were the cheering section. Of course Keaton was there too, but he was expected to be as our deckhand. I stood up on the dock and watched, occasionally taking a picture. To say it was rather exciting, is an understatement!

Right off the git-go Keaton fell in! He stepped up on the spare tire to get a better hold on the boat, but when his weight hit the empty rubber of the flat tire pitched him off into the bay. Shall we say deep enough to hear even quiet Keaton exclaim.

When the boat finally came off the trailer, Bill was by himself in it, and had his hands full. When he got it under control, Keaton and I jumped in and rode around the point to the south harbor with him. The kitties stayed tucked in on the bed until we were secure to the dock.

Home may not be so bad. Will reserve judgment until the first blow, as we are parallel to the wind. This evening was calm and peaceful. The lights on the harbor are really pretty."—- *(excerpt from Jan's journal)*

Some of Our (Mis?) Adventures

Because the door is rounded and the doorway square, the rain has free access to the interior. When we barged the boat, we wrapped everything in plastic and zip-locks. Oft times the weather was bad and we knew the waves up through Clarence Straight could get up to 25' before the barge could find shelter. Expecting everything soaked and lots of water in the boat, we were pleased when it was only about two inches deep.

Not necessarily over confident in life, we lived in the boat on land for nearly a week before finally putting it in the water. Of course my biggest fear was we would sink. Parked outside the bunkhouse, the crew made fun of us as we climbed the ladder in and out of the boat. The day we put her in was typical of the area, blustery and damp. I got pictures and was rewarded with a thousand words.

-—April 25 "The only radio we get is KRBD of Ketchikan. To be polite, their views are not my own. Therefore, no weather forecast."—- *(excerpt from Jan's journal)*

During the first real rain once on the water, we discovered a leak from above and one from below. While I was in Anchorage, both were repaired as best could be done. Bill says working on the boat is like the motorhome, except you can't crawl under it. I won't even go into all the things Bill has repaired, replaced, and just plain added. But, now we can shower and the porta-potty is much better than having none.

As for one of the leaks, it is truly stubborn, so we keep a plastic grocery sack open and laying under these wires that hang at the foot of our 'bed'. Around the windshield-wiper motor is another plastic baggie. When it's raining hard, it fills rather quickly. Imagine waking up with the ceiling less than two feet from your face and a baggy over half full of water hanging above you. Any minute I expect to see a gold fish doing the back-stroke.

Our first real gale was last week. -—April 27 "At 4 AM it was clear and glass calm. By 7 AM it was overcast and waves lapping at the boat. They sounded like the 'boing, dink, plunk' of an old jack-in-the-box. By noon, white caps, gusts, and us were rocking. A healthy gust just hit us. Aside from being rammed against the dock we rode it pretty well. I think. Sure hope the boat and kitties do okay while I'm at work. Can only hope the canvas holds. Feel like a Captain of old writing in his log of the journey. In a way it's true, all except the captain part."—- *(excerpt from Jan's journal)*

Before, when we talked of storms, we might have even mentioned it lasted a few days. No more. Our sheltered existence has ended. I know for a fact; this particular storm blew heavy for a full 49 hours. Count them, forty-nine. We even took several waves over the top of the boat, and we're tied to the dock! *Scary*.

Just think what life might be like to sit at the breakfast table with your cup of tea, and chase it down to have a drink. Or perhaps you don't sleep well lying flat on your back, not to worry, a 45-degree angle can be quite comfy. That is, when you are not seasick. Bill doesn't seem to ever be affected, and I do well on the boat, but the next day at work, I'm woozy for the better part of a day.

One of the Years Pastimes

Making jewelry from fish ear-bones is a big deal and a big seller on the island, so a friend gave me his halibut head. (I understood these were a rather delicate ivory and wanted to try them on a 'dream catcher' pattern I'd heard about.)

Because Bill and I were eating, we told Beau (husband of the cook at the bunkhouse) to put the head at the end of the pier. Besides, it was dusky so the eagles and ravens were already in bed. It would only be a few minutes before I'd put it away so it would be safe until the next morning.

Suddenly Moldie, jumped up and was looking out toward the jetty. I asked her what she was looking at. Bill replied, a wave. Now having just spent 49 hours in REAL rock-n-roll, I wasn't ready for more, I jumped up to see what this wave looked like.

Funny, I thought, I've never seen a foot and a half wave heading *out* to sea before. Then I noticed this wave was being led, by none other than the halibut head!! Can you believe a thieving seal/otter (by now it was too dark to see clearly) had actually come in the basin and STOLE that halibut?!?

Oh well, the next day the *F/V MISKITO* came in with a load of snapper, so I grabbed four of them and got seven of their ear-bones. These weren't delicate, but thick and up to perhaps an inch long. (Later I got ((and *kept*)) another halibut, dissected it but didn't find the bones. So until further instruction, will stick to snapper.)

Another pastime was painting. Last week I had Friday off and painted a picture of a forest fire. Don't ever ask a fisherman about fire, they haven't a clue. Bill thought it was pretty good tho. I entered it in the fair and took second place. Competition was even stiffer than last year, there were only two of us! However, first place truly deserved it, as it was a gorgeous fresh fallen snow scene with new tracks winding through the trees. Regardless, I was able to trade a sunset silhouette painting for two whale tail demitasse cup and saucer with the local gift shop.

Our Furred and Feathered Friends

The eagles have moved in in the past few days. Have you any idea how undignified they sound, with their squeaks and squawks. Despite the noise, it's enjoyable watching them soar. And then laugh when they clump along the sandy strip in minus tides like some stiff, arthritic old man in over starched coat tails. Last weekend a mink came up within four feet of us on the dock before he changed his mind and swam off.

On a recent Sunday tour, we saw a baby bear so little he wasn't as tall as the grass and twin fawns hardly more than two and half feet high. (The deer on the island are small to start with, but these two babies were so tiny.)

October brought us a new dock mate in the form of a very disturbing, tall lanky blue heron. This thing looked absolutely prehistoric with penetrating beady little eyes that have intelligence behind them. When he looks at you, you're left with the distinct impression he knows your innermost thoughts. As he flew around it would remind one of a pterodactyl, all elbows and angles. If he got disturbed in any way, whether he perceived an intentional insult or just another bird flew by, he'd let out the most awful scratchy screech that could send chills down one's spine. Much like the blackboard and fingernail scenario.

As he got more used to our part of the pier, it would be nothing for him to be standing inches away from the window where I sit. He looking in at me and me back at him. Despite his baleful stare, he had the most beautiful amber-colored eyes with a white circle ringing them.

One evening I got mad at Bill for some silly reason and literally threw a temper tantrum, throwing a sack of something out the back door onto the "verandah." Heron must have been right at our window because immediately there was the most startling commotion, squawk great rustling and flap, flap flap! Heron didn't fly away, but attempted to run with those long stilt legs of his. Not immediately knowing what had caused the noise, there were five pairs of eyeballs glued to the window. How startling to see clear amber eyes glaring back at us!

Watching him fish was neat though and I had such fun with Stinkpot. If she was asleep and Heron came round, all I had to do was whisper her name a few times rapidly and she came flying up to see what was out there. If she didn't spy him right away, I would hold her face in its direction until its movement caught her eye. Then her tail would slash back and forth violently.

When Heron would spy a fish, he'd begin to squat down so slowly one didn't see it happen, just that he wasn't standing anymore. How odd and disconcerting to see his legs bending backwards. Soon he'd straighten and a little snippet of fish would be wiggling tight in his beak.

One day though, he must have gotten over confident in his ability to lean down from the dock to the water, a drop of about a foot and a half. Heron started the agonizingly slow downward motion, but something went wrong and he fell between the dock and a boat. Such a screech and he was flapping and trying to climb his way back up on the decking. What a riot to have him turn our way, glare, resettle his feathers as if straightening a shirt and stalk off, all dignity totally destroyed!

It was sad when he no longer came around.

In early November, Bill and I were having before bed cocktails when we heard an unusual thump. After several of them the kitties started acting nervous so we looked out the window to find two otters trying to break in. Their tracks showed that they had been all over the docks in front of us and the skiff beside us. I couldn't believe how big their feet were, at least three inches in diameter.

One day I was visiting with Jan, a fisherman friend, and noticed he had a small rock crab scrabbling slowly across his deck. I asked if he was going to eat it. Jan looked at it for a moment and replied, 'No, I've grown rather fond of the little crustacean. Here, you take him home.' Not really wanting it, I smiled and thanked him, taking it between the back points to avoid the huge claws. With no place to keep it until we decided what to do with it, I stuck it in Bill's beer cooler. Needing to run to the store, I wasn't worried because I would be home in plenty of time before Bill got there.

Need I say I was much later getting home than anticipated?

As I climbed onto the boat, Bill was sitting down with a beer. Saying hi as I began putting things away, he gave a sardonic hi and said 'See this beer?' Yes I said, looking at the beer to see if anything was wrong with it. Bill steadily gave me that look and asked 'Do you know where I got this beer?' Puzzled, I replied, "Of course." Then, "*oh of course!,*" as it dawned on me the location of his beer and the coinciding new resident rock crab.

'Oh my gosh,' I breathed uneasily, 'I'm so sorry! What happened?!' I asked, trying not to laugh aloud. A bit disgruntled, Bill described how he had grabbed for a beer to have something grab back. Jerking his hand out he peered into the beady little eyes of an ugly red thing glaring back at him. Seeing it was a crab; he wondered what I had been doing. Laughing outright now, I told how Jan had given it to us for dinner. Bill looked disgusted and said 'You're not going to cook that little thing are you?' Shrugging my shoulders I said 'I guess not, what do you want to do with it?' He said, 'Why don't we throw it back overboard, after all Sebastian would hardly make for a filling meal.'

Later, whenever we had leftovers Bill didn't want, he'd ask if I'd fed Sebastian the Crab lately, then he'd suggest we give them to him. Sometimes it worked, sometimes it didn't.

An Afternoon in Late June

As I work on this, I'm on the back deck of *ROTORWASH*. Moldie is curled on the cushion beside me and it has begun to rain big fat drops. I love to hear the sound, even on canvas. Stinkpot is living up to her name and trying to escape again. Already I can see the sun pushing clouds aside. Bill worked the morning shift so has the afternoon off. Currently he is scrubbing the boat of algae and other sea life (it grows so fast!).

Last weekend we watched this thing we call a Needle Fish, munch its way along the hull. What a neat creature, long and slender like an eel but with waving fan shaped fins and tail, and a little trumpet shaped nose and face similar to a sea horse. Later we learned its real name was *Bay Pipe Fish*.

Some of the other sea life we enjoy watching around the pilings are: *Pile perch* - fish; *Metridium senile* - frilled sea anemone; *Metridium giganteum* - white-plumed anemone; *Serpula vermicularis* - flowers from the tube (tube worms); also 'flowers' of the class *Polychaeta* a tube worm most similar to the *Christmas Tree Worm Spirobranchus spinosus*, but found only in California. *Ophlitaspongia pennata* - red sponge; *Pisaster ochraceus* - ochre star, the regular starfish; *Asterina miniata* formerly *Patiria miniata* - bat starfish (some of them actually come in blue); *Ceramaster patagonicus* - cookie star, possibly confused with a bat starfish; *Pycnopodia helianthoides* – sunflower star; *Emigrapsus nudus* - beach crab; *Pugettia richii* - kelp crab; *Mopalia* - (mossy) chiton; *Strongylocentrotus droebachiensis*- green sea urchin; *Strongylocentrotus purpuratus* - purple sea urchin; *Parastichopus californicus* - California sea cucumber; *Cyanea capillata* - lion's mane or sea nettle jelly fish; and *Aurelia aurita* - moon jelly fish.

"Excerpts from a letter written by Bill" - June

Greetings from the Bridge of the *M/V ROTORWASH*.

We are in South Harbor 74, Craig, Alaska, which is a better name than the end of the dock.

Boat life is a lot better than we expected. We spent about a week moving in the boat from the van. During this time the boat was still on the trailer in the bunkhouse parking lot.

Our trip up wasn't too bad. We left Portland and went up the Olympic Peninsula to Port Townsend with a stop in Lilliwaup. At Port Townsend we got on the ferry to Whidbey Island, then went to Anacortes and spent the night in the ferry line. The next morning we got on the San Juan ferry and went through the San Juan's [Islands] to Sydney [British Columbia]. It was a real nice trip until we got to Sydney. Customs took quite a while. I must look guilty or like a crook.

Bucchart Gardens was nice. We sniffed flowers and took pictures and walked around in the rain. Then we headed north for Port Hardy. The map of Vancouver Island is not correct. It's 280 miles from Victoria to Port Hardy or about 24 hours of driving. We got to Port Hardy about an hour before the ferry was to load.

The Canadian ferry was like a small ship. The bow lifted on. We just drove on and parked. The ferry ride wasn't too bad, lots of islands to see until dark, then other boats we passed.

Canadian beer is higher percent and sneaks up on you. About 3AM we stopped at Bella Bella and some people got off. Then it was off to Prince Rupert. We got there about 7AM and were glad to get off the boat. Sixteen hours is a long time.

We spent two days in Prince Rupert being tourists and camping in the van. On Tuesday, we boarded another ferry for Ketchikan. The ferry from Prince Rupert to Ketchikan takes six hours and about half way we passed the barge with our equipment on it. I could see the loaders and our fuel truck. I know the boat was in the container pile but couldn't see it.

When we got to Ketchikan some of the crew was waiting and others were coming in. (The helicopter flew by the ferry as we pulled out from Prince

Rupert.) Louis and Paul (both mechanics) took trucks from Ketchikan and we all got on another ferry for Prince of "Whales" Wales Island and as per our normal, there was a storm on Clarence Straight and it was snowing when we got there.

Jan and I spent a couple more days living in the van before the barge with our boat arrived. We moved onto the boat but our slip wasn't ready. A boat on a trailer isn't the ideal RV. And we weren't quite ready for boat life. We were but the boat wasn't. After a week in a parking lot, boat ready or not it was going in the water.

The launch date was set. The slip was ready; the meter was on for power. We figured to launch at high tide because of the problems we had with the trailer at Ten Mile Lake. So Jan and Keaton and I put the boat in the water. Me, being the Captain of the worthy craft, started the engines and began to ease off the trailer, but the boat wouldn't co-operate, so Keaton and I both lifted the bow to unsnag the hook and Keaton fell in. After a little splashing around and other words of encouragement, the launch was a success and we were off on the maiden voyage.

Here I notice the engines aren't getting along too well. In fact the boat didn't want to go straight. One of those Swedes [twin Volvo's] was dead, but restarted without much fuss.

We came into the harbor and headed for the slip, and plowed the dock leaving a black smear on the hull from the tire protecting the dock. Tires do a nice job of protecting a dock, but don't do much for a fresh wash job on a white hull.

By now I've named the engines. Ole is on the left and Sven is on the right, and those two Swedes may never get along.

The throttle cables weren't rigged right and one engine wouldn't idle. A two-engine boat is hard to handle on one.

Like any other motorhome we've had, I had to replumb the water, rebuild the shower drain, and fix the water heater.

We set up house on the dock. It's become quite comfortable. You get to where you don't notice the rocking and the cats have taken over the place.

Fourth of July:

We got four days off in a row. We went fishing, caught no fish, the cats got seasick, Ole blew an oil cooler and Sven is pissing coolant in the bilge.

We pulled the boat out to fix the engines and Jan scraped the hull. Stuff can really grow on the hull. (I waxed it with a tasty combination of wax and jet fuel.)

We spent a couple of days on land and were sure glad to be back on the water. I never noticed how dirty it is on land. Sure track a lot of mud.

Yesterday, a couple of kids were harassing a gray whale with a ski boat. The whale took about all it was going to take, and rammed the boat. Put a good crack in it and knocked one guy in the water. Then, as a parting shot, smashed the windshield with its tail. Everyone survived but the boat is a mess. Don't mess with whales. "End of Excerpt"

One of Bill's Favorite Stories

As told by Bill.

It was a fine bright morning and we were getting ready to take the boat out. We hadn't filled the fuel tanks since we got here, we needed fuel. And as my bride was home that day, I figured it would be a good time to teach her how to be a deckhand. So we unfurled the canvas and cast off from our pier heading for the fuel dock.

As worthy Captain, I had instructed very carefully, telling my wife to do exactly as I say. That is when we got in to the fuel dock to throw the guy the rope. Well, when we got to the dock it was busy so we had to wait. I circled off the end a little bit waiting our turn, I as Captain of the bridge and my faithful deckhand Jan on the deck.

Soon we got cleared. I made an approach to the dock classic style, close in, she could have handed the rope over. But she did exactly as I had instructed and threw the rope. All of it. The poor fuel boy had never had this happen before and he stood there looking at us with both ends of the rope in his hands wondering what he was supposed to do next.

At that time, I realized we were at the dock, in the wind, no power, blowing away. So I did the only thing I could do. I reached out and wrapped my arms around a large piling and pulled us in. In the meantime, all the old weathered salts were standing on the dock above us looking down and laughing their fool heads off.

The fuel boy had the presence to tie the boat to the rope so we couldn't float off again and good old Frank, a fuel truck driver, tied the front. Then we commenced to fuel.

Talking to Frank, I said Jan was a good deckhand because she did exactly what I told her to do. He said it was the first time he'd ever seen a boat tied up from the bridge before.

A Continuation

As told by Jan.

From there we went fishing and things got worse. It wasn't a bad day, a little breezy. But I guess when you are a little kitty in three-foot swells it might seem like a hurricane. When all three were actually green with, well envy isn't exactly the correct word, we knew it was time to go home. Besides we hadn't even had a bite and that's when Ole and Sven decided to go on vacation.

It should be added to the previous story (this written by Jan), that despite the fact we have an electric meter by our slip, we are still in transient moorage. What this means is, if we move the boat it is fair game for anyone else to move into our slip. No matter that the bike is there, the grill is there, or that there is obviously an electric cord running to *something* for some reason.

On putting in to South Cove that day, our worst fears were realized when there was a boat in our space. Along this side of the pier there is only room for five boats anyway and space had been at a premium for some time. Who knows how many boats we had let raft to us already this season.

Fortunately for us, the *F/V SANDRA FAY [Fishing/Vessel]* was out so we pulled in there, preparing to settle in for the night, although I worried what would happen if he came home. As it turned out, that was to become the least of my worries, as that's when Bill found we were taking on water (Ole and Sven's vacation). That is also the weekend we spent in the bunkhouse parking lot scraping hulls and repairing engines.

Of course I know the main thing you want to know is if *SANDRA FAY* came in or not, right? Yes, as a matter of fact he did. Oh you mean us? After the Fourth of July crush, we were able to get back in our slip with minimum rearranging.

That was also the last time we took the boat out too. As Bill put it, 'it was kinda like taking the motorhome to the grocery store.'

Another Fishing Expedition

It wasn't long after the whale attack and our thwarted fishing expedition that Bill and I both had a lovely day off, together. Making the most of it, we grabbed one of the fourteen-foot skiffs and left early one morning.

The sun was glorious on the ocean, leaving dazzles of lights sparkling behind ones' eyes. Heading southwest away from Craig, we puttered along toward San Juan Bautista Island. The day was so nice, it almost didn't matter if we caught anything.

Watching the morning mist fither away and somewhere in a day dream, we both reacted instantly to a sound we seemed to know instinctively. Shielding our eyes and looking toward a small island starboard, we could see the tell-tale signs of a whale spout. With enormous eyes, I asked Bill what it was doing, all the while figuring out how to abandon ship without going overboard.

With a shrug he said it was fishing. Of course the argumentative side of me wouldn't let that go, and I told him I thought whales only ate plankton, not fish. Again he shrugged and kept trolling, in the direction of the whale!

Now bravery comes in all forms. All of which I have *none*. Had Bill made the slightest hint we probably ought not be there, I would have choked and sputtered why weren't we already back in the basin?! But my dear sweet, immovable Bill, just kept motoring forward.

By now, the whale had spouted several more times and we watched as he glided through the calm waters. What a beautiful sight to see the fine spray he cast glistening in the sun. Who could fish when one had such marvelous spectacles to watch?

Well, for one, Bill.

Forcing me to abandon whale watching he made me cast my line overboard. For over three hours the whale and we circled the small island, never more than a few hundred feet apart. Figuring the whale would scare all the fish away, it was exciting when Bill got his first bite. Trying to handle the boat and reel in his line became quite a show. But he did it and landed a seven pound or so, coho salmon.

As if taking turns, the next bite was mine. All along I'd been fussing about how heavy the pole and weights were. Bill said I'd need it to catch anything.

When the bite hit I was taken by surprise and almost lost the pole. The battle of the salmon and combined weight made me sure I had a hundred pounder. Bill again juggled between the boat and *not* trying to help me.

After this, Bill swapped poles with me. Not that we needed to. We each got one more strike but missed each fish. Knowing we were between runs; we were glad we had caught anything. Besides, watching the whale so close and so natural more than made up for lack of fish.

A Different Fishing Expedition

One morning I was driving to Klawock to work, when I noticed a fellow standing at water's edge with a long pole doing something. Curiosity won out and I stopped.

Carefully climbing my way down to him, I watched as he thrust the long pole in, slowly pull it back, stop, then repeat the motion. When I reached the fellow, he didn't even look up. Watching but still not seeing what he was actually doing, I finally had to ask. To my surprise, he was getting sea cucumbers.

Sam, as he introduced himself, showed me the dark red or off purple blobs he was stabbing with the pole, then pulling to shore. When he had several at water's edge he reached down and picked up these disgusting football shapes with limp stickers all over. Here, he showed me how to slice off the head. (I never did figure out which end that was.) Wring out the guts and slit open the belly to reveal the prettiest white-meat fillet. Then simply peel out the little finger steaks. Offering to send some home with me I declined, not because I didn't want them, but because I was late as usual for work and didn't have any way to keep them cool. Thanking him, I assured him I would be out the next low tide I had off.

While it wasn't quite the next low tide, it wasn't many more weeks before it was a pretty morning and I was off for the day. Bill had morning, and was working at a beautiful spot called Sugar Point about fourteen miles away. Checking the tide book, timing would be perfect as I'd be there in about an hour, just after low tide.

When I showed up and told Bill what I was going to do, he shook his head, handed me a garbage sack and a little foot long piece of wire, hooked at one end. Walking down on the beach, I could look out among the little islands a few yards away.

The rock I started on was on the edge of an abyss and felt pretty scary. The tide swirled around my legs and I was certain each influx would try to sweep me away. A sudden snort caused me to nearly jump off the rock before I realized it was a small whale blowing less than thirty feet from me. I watched for about fifteen minutes while he surfaced and blew, swam a ways, surfaced and blew again. What an awesome sight.

Soon I became engrossed in the search for sea cucumbers. From my vantage I could easily see dozens, but they were all out of my reach. Already I was standing in knee deep water, bending out and down as far as I could with that silly wire and they were still feet away.

Not willing to get any closer to the edge than I already was I started working my way back up the side, pulling the sea grass apart and searching under it. This proved profitable when I found three. Just as I got them up and into the garbage sack, Bill came along. I told him how Sam had cleaned them and luckily he took over from there.

When Bill got home that night, he wanted to cook them. The steaks began about the size of my palm, literally with little finger strips. After they came in contact with the heat though, they rolled up like huge round cigars. We figure next time we'd use the ulu and slice them into little strips and cook them that way. The flavor was delicious, very delicate. As Sam had said, they were indeed 'poor man's abalone.'

Attitudes

Monday's we buy the local paper, *The Island News*. Of the eight pages, the front one is devoted to legislative news from Juneau; the second page are Thank Yous' from the community and letters to the editor; the third and fourth pages are where any news might be. Pages five and six are reserved for the police report and court column; and the rest is classifieds and notice of bids on abandoned timber. One particular issue made me doubt my eyes. There buried amongst the junk was a little blurb that Greenpeace would be visiting Prince of Wales.

As a family supported by timber dollars, one must realize where our loyalties lie. To avoid an unwelcome political discussion, I will simply relate that the bank put on a barbecue for the 'peaceful' demonstration held by locals on the docks. Our contributions were banners with a variety of thoughts, several I'll admit unprintable. As *ROTORWASH* was in a highly visible location, there were many remarks by the locals, of which all the ones we heard were in support of our position.

Some of Our Local Color

Jan, on the *F/V KOLA*. This is such an outrageous mangling of a boat, that it almost defies description. Or so we thought. Come to find out it is actually a prototype, one of seven sister ships. With an inch of fiberglass hull hanging underwater and a doorway (the only upright-above-water structure on the boat) in which to enter the front half of the hull, this is where Jan lives. It's a hovel the size of a large shower. He says the hull is good for hitting things at four knots and under, but anything above that and one had better beach it soon. We found out he was in the Navy and had something to do with chemistry, altho for reasons unknown bailed out of the *world*. He water paints outrageous underwater abstract pictures. Until we knew his name, we called him Popeye, a pretty apt description.

Gerald, an electrician, lives on another morphydite, unnamed. It is white, about twenty feet long and square. Almost like a houseboat, minus the house. He is a rigid little fellow that another boater described as 'worrying more than a fart in a frying pan'. We rather liked that one.

This other boater is Juliana, a nurse, and her eye-doctor husband Miles. They live on a beautiful boat named *M/V MISS ALICE*, but we didn't know that, so called it 'Mahogany' because of all the wood. They have a nice black dog named Lucy. Apparently they live a lifestyle similar to ours, but only work in the winter. This year they are being sent to Kentucky. Usually their jobs are in the Midwest. Juliana could be a lot of fun, but Miles is rather intimidating and makes me uncomfortable, so I abandon ship when he comes aboard.

'Cowboy' appears to be a temperamental old hippie but turned out to be an ex-Vietnam Vet with severe flashbacks. He spends his time on the *M/V OLD SMOKEY*. And boy does it! His motor doesn't steer left and on more than one occasion I have seen him ram another boat trying to get in or out of the basin. We were the recipient of this wood to fiberglass kiss at least once. When *OLD SMOKEY* fires up, I sort of hang out on the dock, watching the fish float by. He has a dog, Socks, that hates me as badly as I hate him. He's always trying to bite me or get me to jump off the dock. I in turn try to kick him and get him to bail!

The *F/V LIBBY XII* is a huge boat James Something-or-Other owns. The Harbor Master has been trying to kick him out of south cove for the past season because of his size, but James keeps coming back. He says he likes the folks on this side of the docks as they're 'laid-back and friendlier'.

Rick, on the *F/V SANDRA FAY* is a fish-aholic. Well, maybe that isn't fair, he hates fish and fishing. However, he says he hates the thought of working even worse so his 'job' runs July 15 thru September 15. I asked him how he was able to make enough money to live on for a whole year. He took on a thoughtful look, scratched his head, and said 'I don't'. Apparently he doesn't manage his money well and by mid-March, he says he's broke and living on the boat bumming groceries.

Pete's Papa, who now we know is Oscar, lives on the *F/V LAURA LEANN*. I can't say if it is a motor or fishing vessel, because it never moves. I think his plan is to fix the boat up and go fishing next year. Until I found out Oscar had a stroke this past year, I thought he was an old drunk. As he meandered up the dock with a determined lurching gate I was always worried he'd fall overboard. What I found out is his right foot is numb so he doesn't know when he's connected with the deck. Pete by the way is an <u>old</u> scroungy poodle. But the other day both Pete and Oscar got haircuts and were quite handsome.

The old guy Rob, on the *F/V ZEPHYR* is a cutie. He won't speak to me, but smiles and shyly says 'hi' whenever I walk by.

There has to be a story about Walter on the *F/V OB*, but I have yet to learn it. I don't think he lives on the boat, altho he shows every sign of doing so. I believe he has two grandsons that are always with him and when we rent movies at Radio Shack he is usually there too, with the kids. More often than not, when the boys ask for a movie he says no, because they have the video on the boat. Now go figure.

Hal and Barbara own *F/V MOSKITO*. He used to be an insurance salesman but decided he was getting old before his time and bought a boat. We buy crabs from him, three for $10, most Sunday afternoons.

F/V HYTREK was originally from Newport, Oregon. I'm not sure how George got it here. He owns "Eat-Me Seafoods" where we buy our fish and shrimp. They say opposites attract and he and his wife Sharon, a teacher in Craig, prove that statement. George has been so good to us bringing down buckets of shrimp or salmon fillets. One morning I told him we were real pigs, eating the full five pounds of shrimp he had brought. He laughed and said no, we were only piglets, his wife was a pig after she had eaten ten pounds by herself! George was in Vietnam and has some different ideas but he is a fun fellow to talk with. The name of his business describes his attitude toward the Outside world.

The *M/V MISS MEGAN* is owned by a couple of kids that don't know anything about boating. They come into the harbor usually at full throttle and two guys jump off the boat at the last second and attempt to deflect her from ramming up on the dock. I refer to her as Vessel only, within a week of purchase the fellow had blown a piston. It was lucky for us they were broken down, but oh so spendy a fix for such a young family.

Last, but not least, we have the illustrious A-Hole on the *F/V MIASSIS DRAGON*. In all fairness, up until about two weeks ago the guy would come flying into the harbor and slam up against the dock, causing the kitchen or whatever else to rearrange itself. Well, I was grumpy and looking for a reason to be cranky, so when he came flying in and then left without me being able to yell at him, that really torked me! So I wrote him a nasty note explaining the wake sign and warned him if he didn't slow down I would file a complaint and tacked it to his cleaning table with a knife. Since then he has not only come in quietly, but has even been pleasant.

Wonders the power of the pen, *(pause)* or was the pen mightier than the sword?

Other Color

The scenery on Prince of Wales can be breathtaking. From spectacular flaming sunsets to moonlit nights as bright as day where you can actually see the "rabbit in the moon" skipping across the bay. (I've never been able to see the "man in the moon." I've only ever seen a rabbit. Japanese folklore has a story about a rabbit and the moon.) But the evening the rainbow fell in the water was simply too beautiful to quietly sit back and contemplate.

Jumping in the skiff, we raced out to sea for an even better vantage of God's promise. As we chased the rainbow across the bay it seemed to gently smile and wink at us, reminding us of my Mother's promise. And then, so quickly it was gone. Leaving no trace in the sky, but a comfort in our hearts, as Mother had always promised to be with us whenever we saw a rainbow.

Fiddler on the Dock

One evening, I got home from work around 7 PM. As I was walking down the dock I heard an unfamiliar noise, but it seemed like music. Thinking one of the boats had their stereo turned up, I didn't give it another thought. But as I neared *ROTORWASH*, it got louder and distinctly more like fiddle music. Climbing on the boat, I caught site of a fellow over on the Forest Service docks who was indeed playing a fiddle. Delighted, I dropped the groceries and sat on the edge of the pier listening to this unexpected concert.

After about ten minutes, when it didn't seem like the fellow was going to stop, I got up and poured myself a glass of wine. Over an hour later we both were still there. His repertoire included light hearted jigs and heart wrenching ballads. As I sat behind a piling he couldn't see me, so when he quit and started to leave I applauded. Quite surprised, he finally noticed me and tipped his head in acknowledgment.

The fellow played once or twice more, but that evening was the most enjoyable. Several weeks went by and I never saw him again. Finally, I went over and asked who he'd been. Turns out he was one of the fellows brought in to supervise building of the new offices. Playing the fiddle was his way of relaxing. I told them we sure enjoyed it. They agreed.

Holidays

-—July 24 - Our 13th Anniversary! We went to Thorne Bay for the Prince of Wales Fair and Logging Show. The weather was hot, but beautiful. My painting of the fire took second... When we got home we were <u>so</u> dusty we decided to indulge in a shower ($3 for 10 minutes) up at the Harbormaster's. But alas no luck, they closed at 9 PM, it was 9:05 PM. Bill got a home shower, then the water line blew out, so I wiped down but my hair is still a mess! For our anniversary Bill got me a pair of scrimshaw ivory earrings with an iris painted on them. They are real pretty. I got him a book of poems by Robert Service. -—*(excerpt from Jan's journal)*

-—July 27 - Bill's 47th Birthday. For the first time I can remember he was excited about his day. It made me very glad. Weather's been back to normal the last few days and it's rainy. Bill had a lovely birthday. He had morning, so I raced around decorating. Couldn't find the cards I'd gotten him so after work I picked up a few more, his cake and ice cream, then came home and baked it. Earlier I'd wrapped a four-set Patrick McManus books-on-cassette, and money for a ten-minute shower. He laughed when he opened the quarters, he'd never received a shower before.

Dad called the service van to wish us a happy Anniversary. He'd confused the 24th with the 27th, but that was all right.—- *(excerpt from Jan's journal)*

The Storm

-—August 27 - "For the first time since February 1988, we went camping! Took off and drove up the island to El Capitan. Found Memorial Beach. It was named after the twelve people killed when their Otter went down for no apparent reason in Sumner Sound. It was beautiful, not sandy, but a mile or so of fine pebbles, and of course it certainly didn't hurt matters that a whale sounded right off the beach.

Weren't able to camp there but drove back south about ten miles. Found a rock pit and made dinner. Then we read the newspaper until dark, fired up the lights and played Uno. Bill whipped me soundly. It was a beautiful clear night but not cold. Earlier, we'd seen a deer and a bear. The drive was long and dusty but relaxing." -—*(excerpt from Jan's journal)*

September 8 - A Week Later

Life on the *ROTORWASH* seems to be a continuing saga. Or is our life the saga? Sometimes one can never tell. Things had been pretty mellow from the Fourth of July until last weekend, when we got our first gale of the autumn season.

It was rather amusing, a few weeks ago I spoke with my niece. She told me my sister Ruth was all excited, trying to get through to us on the radio phone. This was because Prince of Wales and Southeast had been hit by a tremendous storm with ferocious winds and driving rain. Calmly, I explained to her that Ruth must have us confused with another country as we had had some rain, but, *(scoff)* nothing to even notice. When I got home and relayed all this to Bill, we both had a laugh. Then we discussed some of the local fellows who were out fishing, namely the *KOLA, OB* and *ZEPHYR*, and wondered if they had noticed anything untoward.

As it turned out, they all came in before the holiday weekend. Although we didn't chat with the *OB* or *ZEPHYR*, we did talk with Jan and asked how the weather had been. He said it was pretty weird with lots of thunderstorms. Looking at the design of his boat, I asked if it had been exciting. Sheepishly he grinned and said yes. We told him Ruth's tale and all laughed about her paranoia.

Because it was the holiday, Bill, Keaton, Jake, and Liam (two other mechanics), and I were all going up to the north end of the island and go camping. The weekend before, we had found a beautiful little beach that we thought would be fun to sleep on.

Loading gear and guys, we were off. Because Keaton is our normal baby-sitter, we asked Ted from another boat to watch the kitties. Taking his responsibilities seriously, he asked lots of questions about their personalities; was there anything they liked better than something else; would there be enough food; (we were only going for two nights); how often ... and on, and *on*, and ON!

El Capitan is the longest mapped cave in Alaska, with more than 11,000′ of passage. This year, more than 3,000 caves have been found to be part of this system. Although the locals had always known of its existence, the Forest

Service didn't 'discover' it until 1988, when they began their research of the cave system.

Thus, being the brave ones we are, we decided to go spelunking. Long story short, it was a mere 365 stairs, not steps, UP to the entrance. I thought Keaton was going to die around step number twenty. Once there, an ominous sign encourages entrance with words of danger, Caution, EXPERIENCED ONLY, *FLASH FLOODS*, **SURVIVAL GEAR!**, etc. Armed with flashlights (and I even had a soled pair of water walkers on) we entered the darkness.

Around the tenth boulder we had to scramble over, we were in the dark. Jake was in the lead, but somehow Bill was the one to find the first overhang. Fortunately, he had already broken his glasses while in Burma, so the damage was only to his nose. With words of warning echoing around, I found the overhang next. But a perceptive sixth sense stopped me less than an inch from a new nose. Keaton stopped short of a huge sinkhole about ten feet wide and easily fifty feet deep. But, by the twentieth boulder or so, we opened onto a wide sandy path that began to lead us down into the bowels of the earth.

While I'd like to make the rest of the story exciting, I can't. The cave ended within another fifty feet at a monstrous iron gate work. But the cave was cool (sorry)! There was evidence of stalactites, mini ones anywhere from a half inch to three inches. And if I were to be a vandal, there was this beautiful white frothy rock that ran in a short wave away from one overhang. I know it would look gorgeous on the mantel at home in Oregon.

The weather by then had turned cool and breezy. Jake was convinced it was going to rain so he and Liam headed back to Craig. As we were already three hours from home, and I wanted to pick high bush cranberries to try and make ketchup, we headed on up the island. That day we saw a bear that actually curled its lips at us like in the movies, five deer, one helicopter logging (not ours), and a seal.

Where we'd wanted to camp on the beach was full by the time we got there. Now what makes the bit about it being full so amusing, is our 'highway' is a fairly rough dirt road. For over two and a half hours fifteen miles per hour is too fast for the ruts and chug holes. The remaining two and a half hours is at the breath-taking speed of thirty. Labouchere Bay is a mere seven miles from this beach but whoever goes where one lives? Plus, now there were very few people left since Ketchikan Pulp pulled out because of mill closures.

So this means the only ones to venture forth are from the south end, like us. Sure enough the folk there, all three parties we knew, all from Craig. But this also means there were only about twenty people at the north end of Prince Of Wales Island.

A few miles up the road we picked our spot. Keaton lost the coin toss and had to cook dinner. Bill set up the tent for us to sleep in. (Originally, when Jake and Liam were with us, Bill and I were going to sleep in the van and the three fellows sleep outside. But in all fairness, I didn't feel right making Keaton sleep out by himself.) This gave me the time to go blueberry and high-bush cranberry picking, always within sight of camp I might add. As I have said many times, I am not brave. This is a fact I am not ashamed to admit. Keep in mind too, we live on one of the most highly bear populated islands in the entire southeast of Alaska!

After dinner and a vicious game of *Uno,* it was time for bed. All through the game I had been trying to graciously find a way to not have to sleep outside. We talked about the bear we had seen earlier. (Although there wasn't sign of any within two or three miles.) Then we talked about the deer prints behind the van. The ones that showed a fair-size buck in rut. (As we had had heavy rains a few days earlier this meant the little beggar had been there recently.) We didn't talk about space men, but the thought crossed my mind.

Bill drug out our warped toothbrushes (I tried to sterilize them one time and the bristles melted) and handed me mine. It was now or never to declare my stand and say NO, I would NOT sleep out there with all those scary Lions and Tigers and BEARS! But did I? No! That would have been too easy, instead I meekly took my toothbrush and stood looking at the stars, listening to the wind rustle the leaves, and trying desperately not to THINK!!

We climbed into our bed, a very poor imitation of the soft cushions on the boat. Bill looked at me (I'm sure I saw a nasty gleam in his eye) and asked innocently if I was ready for the flashlights to go out. Bravely I said yes. Snuggling as close to him as possible, I settled in for a very... long.... night.

Well, to reward your patience with this long tirade, it wasn't but a few minutes before our first bit of excitement occurred. The wind was still whispering ominously in the trees and (unfortunately) we could hear everything around us very clearly. Suddenly, the crashing of rocks brought Bill straight up in bed and me diving under the pillow. Instantly, his hand flashed at the side of the tent. Immediately he was lying back on his pillow, squishing me. Fearing the worst, I squeaked what was it?! In a grave voice, he whispered, "A mouse."

Well.

Back to the snuggle position we went.

Again your patience will be rewarded when within another few minutes, MORE rocks crashed. This time Bill tightened his grip on me as I was preparing to flee. We lay there silently, letting our ears warn us of the impending danger.

Silence.

That's it. Silence. Some rocks had fallen.

Well!

It was at this point I asked Bill if he wasn't ready to move inside yet. That voice that I have come to know and dislike so intensely, the one that brooks no challenges, responded, No.

I knew this couldn't go on. Willing myself to relax, I was dismayed to hear Bill's breathing return to normal, then slow and finally become the rhythmic sigh of sleep. While it is totally unfair of me, I desperately did not want to be awake by myself. Furthermore, I wanted to be asleep before him, so HE could be the one to hear whatever was going to get us next. Surprisingly, all this worry and concentration about his breathing put me to sleep.

But you know it didn't last.

Sleep had come, but the subconscious was ever on the alert. Time isn't relevant but it couldn't have been more than fifteen minutes when Bill stiffened and whispered in a voice filled with real graveness 'Did you hear that?' Unfortunately, yes I had. A dreaded soft scrape and most unwelcome snort.

Now I ask you, what did we expect? Here we are, living on an island with thousands of bears and all they can do is multiply. WHAT DID WE EXPECT??!! Worse, fools that we are, we are attempting to sleep in a tent, a puny little, thin clothed, absolutely no protection, TENT!! And to top it off, the safety of our roomy, thick-metal walled van is a mere few feet away.

I REPEAT, *what did we expect?!*

While all of this is racing through my brain, Bill is trying to pull pants on, turn on flashlights, get the tent open, and check out what made that dreadful noise. Me, well, I'm trying to find a way to get <u>under</u> the sleeping bag. Remember, I have already admitted to being a coward here.

It was an eternity of perhaps ten seconds and Bill returned to report, that yes, a deer had attempted to, wait, what? a deer?, deer isn't pronounced b-e-a-r. What do you mean, deer? All this worry about bears, and you are trying to tell me a deer brushed past our tent, didn't like the way we smelled, and snorted??

WELL!

Once again we lay down. I attempted to feint sleep, but of course my mind is full of visions of bear dancing on our tent. Bill's breathing is once again leaving me behind. Waking him, I said I just wanted to let him know I didn't want him to worry about me; I told him, that he didn't have to ask if I was ready to move in yet; that he could decide for us to go inside anytime and not ask my opinion; that it would be totally OK with me if we moved in to the van; that... He said, "Do you want to move in?" Already out the door, I turned, looked back and said, "I thought you'd never ask."

Poor Keaton, he never even knew there were adventures right outside his door. He had slept through everything, missing it all. We didn't want to worry him either, so we told him it had started to rain and we were getting wet.

Settling in, it wasn't but a few minutes before Bill was sound asleep and snoring softly. Just drifting off I heard an odd noise. Laying on my belly, I lifted my head, turning my ear to get a better sound. This new noise didn't have me frightened, I was safe in the van now, only curious. It was rather a deep resounding clunk, clunk, clunk. Much like the sound of a bear trying to push over a tree. After several more minutes I still wasn't able to identify it, so I woke Bill.

Whispering I wasn't frightened, but would he please listen and tell me what that was? In a few seconds, he said it was Keaton snoring. No, I said, it doesn't sound at all like a snore, listen closer. Bill told me to turn over, when I did, sure enough, Keaton was making the funniest little conk, conk noise we'd ever heard. Giggling, soon we too were asleep.

The next morning, it truly was raining. A quick breakfast and we started back south. One bear and nineteen deer later, we pulled into Craig in a fine gale.

Within minutes, Ted had come to the door raving about how bad the wind and waves had been earlier and more were expected. He said at one point there were waves inside the harbor over a foot and a half high. He said he even noticed a few crossing our bow, but that while we had been gone *F/V CAPT. COWBOY* had rafted to us and that protected us for the most part. However, the wind was driving our boat up on the dock so he had had to round up spare buoys to put on us. We thanked him and were extremely happy we'd missed it.

Two action-packed movies and popcorn later, it was bedtime.

Morning came, but tranquility was not to be ours. The next thing we know someone is pounding on the boat and shouting something about 'sinking'! Coming full awake we immediately realized the storm had come up again and once more we were part of the ocean rhythm. My mind raced to us sinking, and while untangling myself from that tiny doorway of the V-Berth, I planned our escape. The kitties go first, next the computer and poinsettia and then financial papers.

As I straighten, the first thing I notice is how dry the floor is, and stop to ponder this phenomenon. The second thing I notice is how quickly Bill can flatten me into the woodwork as he plows over me heading overboard. Well, okay, so maybe he was really trying to find out what Ted was shouting about, but at that moment I was sure he was abandoning ship!

Too soon we discovered, with the return of storm winds, the *MISS MEGAN* had been stern into the wind and taken on water. The only thing holding her up was the tie downs. As the Harbor Master didn't have the equipment to do anything, Bill and I jumped in a company truck and ran to the service landing for pump, inner tubes, ropes, and the generator.

By the time we got back quite an audience had accumulated. It took Bill, Jan, Miles off the *M/V LADY ALICE,* and Gerald almost four hours to float *MISS MEGAN* again. What a mess! All that engine oil was inside the cabin, on the curtains, walls, and floors.

Thinking our adventures had ended for the day, we came home and Bill started cooking breakfast. Too soon he shouted 'Holy Sh__!' Knowing it was our turn to sink, I shouted What?! He shouted back 'Look at that log!' And out the door he ran. I jumped up and looked out the window and was shocked to see about a twenty-foot cedar bearing down on us.

All this time, the wind and rain kept hammering at us. As we drank our tea, the cup was never more than half full. The pens on the table were laid sideways, and the stack of videos was spread one layer thick, while we rocked with the rage of the sea.

Now the basin we live in is quite open. When we first saw the log it was barely inside the jetty. But by the time Bill was able to run to the skiff, get it started and come alongside the log, it was already battering into *M/V DADS KNEE*, tied up in front of us.

As Bill is such a hero, he went this entire rescue mission alone. Although in truth the situation was by no means funny, I liked to laugh myself silly watching him attempt to duck the rain, shield the wind, keep the skiff in motion *but* keep from ramming *DADS KNEE* too, lasso the log, <u>*and*</u> start towing his own log deck of one, back to sea!!

At one point he was in the jetty opening and then that pesky log would escape and head straight for us. Next, Bill would be wind driven against the piling in the corner of the dock and the log would be ramming him. Then he would be towing the log toward shore and in the next instant it would be towing him toward the dock. He pulled the log bow into the wind and then he towed it stern forward. Soon this too drew quite a crowd. All in all this timber tackle took over an hour. By the time he got back in, he was soaked and fairly frozen.

Although I was still snickering, I told him it would have been a whole lot easier if he would have waited the two seconds for me to grab my shoes and gone with him. The glance he cast my way would never have been misinterpreted as endearing. My hero.

Thus the adventures of the day and weekend were over. We had found Ruth's storm, or perhaps it had found us.

How *Not* to Scrape a Hull

It was a fair day in Craig terms. The rain wasn't hammering, the wind was a steady breeze, and the temperature was fairly mild, easily in the low fifties. So Bill decided it was necessary to begin clear-cutting the jungle accumulating on the hull.

Over twenty years ago Bill used to do underwater welding and still had his original wetsuit. This day, he poured himself into the black, cracked, and dry, representation of rubber. The local dive shop was very modern in their selection of colors. And the neon pink face mask Bill was able to purchase was quite an accessory to his ocean ensemble including neon blue water sox.

While I tried to compose my features into those of a loving, supportive wife, my lips were straining to hold back the gales of giggles as this aberration in black struggled to zip the remaining few inches of stuffed wetsuit. Casting me a grim glare, Bill unzipped the canvas and attempted to step over the side in his second skin.

This is no lie and can be corroborated (albeit reluctantly by the party in question) by our masked madman, but a seagull was sitting on the piling next to the boat. Not that that was so remarkable. But as Bill stepped over the side, this winged-one glanced down to see if food was involved. When it decided there wasn't, it began to glance away but couldn't believe what it saw and quickly looked back again, upsetting its balance and nearly falling off the piling. And then immediately, it began to laugh.

Now laugh you say, pooh. Perhaps you feel generous and will admit that it may have given its raucous cackle, but laugh? Not hardly. Well, we are here to say, this is no fairy tale and this is no war story, laugh it did. Not just a simple chuckle, but a very long, drawn-out belly laugh if you will. One that continued for several minutes. Ending only when the side-splitting spasm caused the silly bird to actually fall off the piling and fly away in mid-amusement, laughing as it went!

Glaring in my direction as I became totally uncomposed, Bill began laughing too when he saw the humor in the bird's attitude. Waddling away, he climbed down onto an inner-tube. As his rubber buns hit the water, the cracks in his antiquated wetsuit filled with forty degrees of reminder why he'd given up underwater welding in the first place. The remarks he made are unprintable, as we consider this piece to be a family story. Yet it can be claimed that a record was set in the length of time it takes one to scrape a healthy hull.

(It might be added that the color of blue on his water sox was only slightly brighter than the color of his lips and hands!)

"Excerpts from a letter" - September 24

Trying to Explain Why We Love it Here.

"We're fine and floating still. Although with all the storms since the beginning of the month, we're pretty damp. I believe *ROTORWASH* came with time-release leaks. Immediately, when we get one stopped and get used to being dry again, another starts. Today's leak is at bed level, just a rivulet under our cushions, enough to keep the sheets soaked. Ugh.

Your simple and perhaps even innocent statement, 'you would like to see the country that keeps us coming back despite, ...', has caused us to spend hours and hours arguing, discussing, disagreeing, pondering, and occasionally coming to a compromise of thoughts.

The second we read that, the answer was so simple, it isn't what the country has, so much as what it doesn't have. Crime is quickest to come to mind. Sure there is some vandalism here, but rape and murder, kidnapping, etc., are virtually non-existent. It would be too difficult to escape the island and everyone knows everyone. Thinking that was pretty easy, end of return letter. Then Bill mentioned this and I mentioned that and pretty soon, the answer wasn't simple anymore. So rather than reply hastily, we talked about it some more.

Then the weekend before Labor Day we drove to the north end of the island. Memorial Beach is only a rock beach, but sweeps around for almost a mile overlooking Sumner Sound. While we stood there listening to the silence, it was suddenly broken by a whale blowing off the beach less than a hundred feet. The sun on the snowcapped mountains in the background, then glimmering on each droplet as it shimmered to the sea was nature at its finest. Truly breathtaking.

A four-plus hour trip at fifteen to thirty miles per hour gives one plenty of time to think. I had pretty well formulated a reply, again expounding on what isn't here, when Bill hit the brakes in time to keep from hitting a mama bear and tiny, baby boo-boo. When the second baby popped over the edge of the road my thoughts were swiftly transformed into 'Well ...'. Then abruptly Bill skidded to a complete stop as the tiniest triplet ran up on the road and slid to a stop, falling on his bottom right there in front of us. He sat there looking up, then quickly got up and ran after his family.

We laughed and talked of this for miles. Then a funny thought caught me as we passed mile-marker 107. Yelling for Bill to stop, I jumped out and took a picture of our "highway" (and the marker in honor of the Vertol). We giggled at the peacefulness of a deserted dirt road.

It wasn't too many more miles before we came across a scroungy guy packing a gun, equally dirty girl, and two mangy mutts. They were hitch hiking, and of course we stopped and picked them up. They had no more gotten in the van than Bill turned to me and lifted his eyebrows. I knew what he was thinking, how are we ever going to explain this!

Turned out they had been fishing and when they were ready to leave, they found they had a flat tire, so were hitch hiking back to Coffman Cove, perhaps fifteen miles away. Not many miles up the road was an abandoned car with tires their size, so we stripped one (the only one not flat can you believe?) and away they/we went.

Here, to carry a gun is the only sensible thing to do with all the bears and several packs of wolves. To pick up someone on foot is a must. (Don't worry, once we leave the island we wouldn't even consider picking up a hitch hiker.)

Suddenly the answer was even more complex. Okay, so now it includes some things that are here too. This newest idea brought days more discussion, to today's date October 16.

As we sit here on the verandah sipping wine and being warmed by *Mr. Heater*, Bill is on the deck fiddling with something, the kitties are snoozing, and the wind is blowing like a banshee. We have seen the sun three times this *month*, which includes less than two hours today. A storm blew in yesterday afternoon and the winds last night were well above forty miles per hour. The boat doesn't do too bad. The canvas pops and leans in the wind, but so far, everything has held together.

Despite our love of this island, six months is a really long time to be anywhere. Especially somewhere the sun doesn't shine often and it is colder and more damp than reasonable. The second storm of September was enough of a blow to stir the water around and drive the floor temperature down at least ten degrees. More often than not you'll find both of us with socks on if we have to stand down on the deck.

Back to the original theme. The people here are pleasant. Life is laid back, something Bill is very good at. The country is pretty and we don't readily have to deal with the mundane essence of living 'somewhere.' Sure we have to pay bills and cook dinner, but two weekends ago Bill had to go in search of a service landing. (As opposed to the log landing, there is a service landing. This is where the helicopter and service van (where the mechanic's keep their tools and parts) are parked, as well as the Night Watch RV or camper.)

It was Sunday, so we ran by the new grocery store, got espresso, sweet rolls, and the *Weekend Edition* to go. Through the course of an all-day drive we saw six bear. A set of twins and mama, one sitting on a log watching what we were doing, and an old gray grizzled one lying in a sun spot. Then there was one that had a ridiculous looking branch of yellow leaves on his head.

Up on top of this one hill the view of the surrounding islands to the west was spectacular.

So it turned out to be an answer we could not easily define. We do know that when Columbia no longer brings us back here, we will have lost a place special to our hearts.

A Day in Bill's Life

(Warning - this next section should not be tried at home for keeping a happy marriage together.)

Pilots can be such whiners at times. The worst ones are those that rarely complain, so when they do, one must act on their whims as soon as possible. This particular day was as the year seemed to be going, a nasty, cold, driving rain, and heavy gusting winds. Ozzie, the Project Manager (PM), called the day (as in shut everything down and stopped logging) by two in the afternoon, but before the pilots left, the command pilot Giles complained that one of the light bulbs overhead was out. Bill promised to fix it before morning.

Running out in the rain, Bill wanted nothing more than to go home, fix a hot toddy, and dry out. Yanking the old light out, he put the new one in and immediately heard an unhealthy *fizzst*. Closing his eyes and taking a deep breath, he thought over what that could have been. Reluctantly, opening his eyes, he knew beyond a doubt the wiring harness had shorted out.

As it was not too much past lunch, and everyone was trying to get hours, there was a full crew of mechanics. They each began taking sections of the harness, cutting out the burned section, and rewiring in a new one. It was a long and tedious job.

By 6 PM, Bill knew he needed to call someone from the shop in Aurora, Oregon, and let them know they would need to send a new harness up as soon as possible. He also wanted to yell at someone for not having put a fuse in the only wire that burned out, which would have stopped the problem hundreds of feet of wire sooner.

Without a thought of his nearby wife, by 7 PM Bill was grabbing a bite to eat at the bunkhouse. He knew this was going to be a very long night. Driving the fourteen miles of rutted road back to the landing, Bill's thoughts returned to the wiring harness and how the short could have been avoided.

As usual, after Jan got home from work she figured out what to cook for dinner and began it around 8 PM to have done by 9 or 9:30 at the latest. This night, a thick soup was in order because the weather was so nasty. When 10 and 11 PM both came and went, Jan wondered what might have happened. After midnight and 1 AM were soon turning to 2 AM Jan became worried. Although the road to the landing wasn't bad, there was a short section of several hundred feet sheer cliff where the road sloped appreciably toward the ocean. In heavy rains such as these, it became a slight river rushing down the center.

Unable to get through on the radio phone, Jan went up to the phone booth and tried to reach the landing. When there was no answer, she decided to drive out to see if perhaps, God forbid, something had happened and perhaps one of the trucks had gone off the road at this section. Climbing into the van with dim headlights that shorted out at each bump and windshield wipers that pondered each swipe, Jan set off in the driving storm.

Bill, Keaton, Jake, and Liam kept at the harness through the night. By 3 AM, they were all bleary eyed, but the end was in sight. Bill and Keaton had had morning the day before so had been on the job nearly twenty-four hours. Out of the gloom headlights shown. Bill glanced at his watch, fearing it was later than he thought and the morning pilots were showing up without the helicopter flyable. Never had any helicopter he had been Crew Chief or Crew on missed a take-off because of maintenance. When he saw it was only Jan in the van, he continued working on the section he was rewiring.

When Jan saw that all the trucks were there and the guys were obviously working on the helicopter, she sent a swift Thank-You heavenward. And then she became extremely angry. Why couldn't someone have let her know that it would be an all-niter.

Walking across the landing, Jan climbed into the helicopter where Bill and the rest of the mechanics were. Everyone was standing there watching what Bill was doing. Bill took one look at Jan's face and told the guys they could all go home to get at least an hour sleep. Immediately, the fellows abandoned the helicopter like rats deserting a sinking ship. All of them mumbled a quick good-night and beat feet, avoiding a direct look at Jan.

Attempting a levity that certainly wasn't there, Bill tried to joke about how long the job had taken. Not even speaking to him, Jan crossed her arms and stood waiting for him to finish as he had no ride home now because the guys had left with the trucks. Bill made the further mistake of mentioning he'd been in town earlier in the evening. Disbelieving he could be so callous with her feelings, Jan looked at him like some disgusting amoeba under a microscope that one is trying to dispose of.

Being smart enough to know he had wandered onto thin karst, Bill didn't try to talk to Jan anymore, but finished rewiring the last of the harness. He did explain that he had simply tried to change a little tiny light bulb early in the afternoon, and this was the result of that temper tantrum. Pretending he didn't exist, Jan never spoke, but quietly sat in the van while Bill drove back to the boat.

By now it was nearing 4:30 AM. As they climbed in the cabin of the boat, Bill commented that dinner smelled good. Giving him a derogatory glare, Jan sat on the couch while Bill changed clothes then dished himself something to eat. Finished by 5 AM, Bill tried to kiss Jan hello/good-bye as he left to return to the landing. A cold cheek was reluctantly offered.

Knowing he had made a slight faux pas; Bill spent the next several days acting contrite and trying to be overly helpful and friendly. While Jan never cut him any slack, she also didn't demand any diamond rings or gold nugget jewelry while he was being so generous.

A Better Day in Bill's Life?

-—April 19 - "Bill had an interesting day, to begin with, he backed all the way to the landing (eight plus miles)! because the transmission went out in the Bronco. Then Keaton had to walk out from the nurse landing, where they fuel the helicopter, because someone blasted a rock pit and the nurse truck was on the other side of a slide on a dead-end road!" -—*(excerpt from Jan's journal)*

Then another time, Bill came home from work with an unbelievable story. A pilot had smashed in our night watchman's camper with the hook!

The hook is an external cargo hook that's a heavy, electrical and mechanical device attached to the belly of the helicopter with a steel cable and electrical cable. (The steel cable, or 'longline,' can be anywhere from 50' to 250' long, thus called a longline.) The hook hangs at the end of the longline. The hookers in the woods attach the choker cables to the hook. (Thus called 'hookers.') The lifting capacity of its capabilities is about 20,000 pounds. When the pilot gets to the log landing he electrically opens the hook so the chokers attached to the logs can drop to the ground.

This particular log landing, the one Bill and I had spent a Sunday finding, was located three quarters up a mountain referred to as Ice House. The road was so steep, it was actually illegal with a 26% grade. The landing itself was crammed into a rock quarry that had been carved out of the mountain. Between the service van, helicopter, and Hank's camper, there was room for nothing else. The road side of the landing had a beautiful view out over Klawock Lake. The rear view, if you will, was a shear rock face, about fifty feet high.

For whatever reasons, this pilot was unable to land by flying in over the top of the quarry and setting down the hook. Both his departures and arrivals were noted by either smashing the hook into the cliff and then dragging it up and over, or the reverse, by slamming it into the ground above and then yanking it over the edge. Neither way safe, but apparently his only way.

This particular day he appeared to be trying a new approach, with disastrous results. As he came in over the landing, he dropped the hook through the top of Hank's camper, then drug it across, ripping off every vent and cover.

Fortunately, his wife Levinia wasn't there, because it hit directly where she usually sits and would have surely broken her neck. As it was, Hank had been standing near the back door. When the roof caved in, it slammed him into the table, bashing his elbow. God was with him, for that was the most serious of his injuries. Hank's humor allowed him to see the similarities between this incident and when a hand grenade goes off inside a tank.

As an after-fact, folk were reprimanded for the location of the landing rather than who caused the damage. It was pointed out this was the only landing available and not the first time it had been used in the past four years either. The issue became moot.

Still another time, late in the season, the Black Bear Hydroelectric Plant still had a long way to go before completion. Despite Columbia's busy schedule flying between the two Native Corporations, Shaan Seet and Klawock Heenya. Ozzie had bent over backwards to try to accommodate lift jobs for the crew constructing the dam.

Unfortunately, after several months it didn't appear Columbia was getting paid very regularly and the fellow was becoming much more demanding of time. To top that, it wasn't uncommon for the helicopter to arrive on the job to find the load exceeded the weight limits. Bill or Jake would explain again the helicopter was rated for 9,500 pounds, cut the load. The guy would whine that it was only a little over, at 11,000 pounds. Unwilling to bend federal regulations they would say NO, cut the load, and dismantling would begin.

The weather had been nasty all year, but this particular day it had clagged in, clouds low, dumping mixed snow and rain. Giles was pilot for the lift. Bill drove out to the staging area and looked over the load then radioed to Giles to come on in. Besides a generator and general supplies, the fellow said there was also food going up to the guys stationed on top of the mountain. He indicated things like milk and bread but several cases of eggs too, so be extra careful.

Flying between a fluctuating ceiling, Giles took the loads as the fellow and Bill hooked them. The last load the guy wanted was the food. Because of the storm, the sky was fast growing dark. With a distinctly lowered ceiling they hooked the eggs and Giles took off trying to talk with the man on top of the hill to see how much clearance he still had. Before Giles was about to crest over the rim of the waterfall, the guy turned to Bill and laughed a little nervously and said, 'you know those eggs were really dynamite.' By then it was too late for Bill to warn Giles.

Furious with the guy, Bill strained toward the radio trying to hear better. Transmission was intermittent but he could follow most of what Giles was saying. As Giles topped the ridge, the ceiling dropped and the load was barely above the tree tops. Suddenly, the radio crackled out a mans garbled yell, 'Look out, pull up, you'll get tangled in those guide wires!' 'What guide wires?!' Giles and Bill both shouted at the same time!

Bill leaned into the little ferret-faced man beside him and growled above the weather, 'You didn't say anything about guide wires!' Still nervous, he hunched his shoulders and said, 'Yeah, just above the lip of the waterfall.'

Although it had been tense, Giles settled the load and took off for the service landing before the mountain range became impassable. Bill looked at the guy, shook his head, and drove off.

It wasn't long after this, the radio phone in the van rang one morning and it was that same guy. With disbelief Ozzie looked at the phone as if he could see the jerk that had the gall to ask for their help again. As it was an open channel, while the guy wheedled for them to do one last lift, a familiar voice broke in. An ex-pilot from Columbia, said his Company could do the job no problem and for even less money. The guy was delighted and they made arrangements, seeming to forget it was on Columbia's line.

Well, as they say, what goes around comes around. As was related by a reliable outside source, the day of the lift the competition arrived to find the load exceeded their lift *capacity*, not even legality. They couldn't do the job after all. Soon the guy had the audacity to call Columbia again. This time, Ozzie told him not to even bother calling back.

Tsunami Tuesday - October 4

The morning had begun peaceful enough. I was drinking my usual morning cup of tea, reading and Bill was still deep in slumber. The shrill screech of the radio-phone brought Bill up and the kitties looking around anxiously. Giles was on the phone calling Jake to warn him a *tsunami* was on the way, due to hit here about 1PM. Both Bill and I looked at each other like this was some sort of weird joke on Giles' part.

Although through the years on rare occasion I had heard about tidal waves, I didn't know anything about them until two days earlier when Bill brought home a *Readers Digest*. Coincidentally, there was an article on *tsunami's* (Japanese for harbor waves). The information was rather scary, and in fact, that night I had had a nightmare about us being in a *tsunami*. It took a long while before I calmed down enough to go back to sleep.

Giles went on to say there had been an earthquake in Japan, magnitude 8.2 at 5:23 AM Alaska time. He was calling to let Jake know that an evacuation of all low-lying areas was in effect. He laughed and told Jake they'd throw tie downs on his trailer, but seriously, he wanted to have him pick up all the saws that were laying around.

With concern not only for ourselves, we worried about our daughter Allison, stationed in Japan in the Air Force. Later we learned she had slept through the entire thing and that the earthquake had hit the northern end of Japan, rather than Yokota.

Bill assured me we didn't have anything to be worried about. I, however, wasn't convinced. Didn't these things generate more wave action as they went? Bill said yes, but by the time the wave hit our outer islands, it would defuse nicely, and we shouldn't get anything more than an influx of water.

Earlier that morning I had seen Nick, the Harbor Master, walking the docks looking at all the boats. I wondered if this was why, then reasoned if there were cause for us to worry, surely he would tell us, wouldn't he?

Not happy to just sit and wait for any unknown thing, I went up and spoke with him. He said the Coast Guard had to issue warnings because if they didn't and anything went wrong, then of course they would be in deep *kimchee*. I asked if it was possible we would get a wave, say fifty-foot proportions. He said while it was possible, it was highly unlikely. Even during the 1964 earthquake, all that had happened was an increase in tidal activity. He went on to explain it would be like the tide running every twenty minutes, rather than six hours, and it could go on for an hour or so. Furthermore, at this moment, whatever was going to happen would be happening in the Aleutians right then. If we were in any great danger, within a half hour fire engines would come around making announcements.

Still not convinced, I flat out asked if I needed to get the kitties and me off the boat. He said no, not to worry, I would see the boats rise and fall around us and should keep the radio tuned to the VHF channel. Thanking him, I went back to tell Bill the news.

As it was time for Bill to go to work, he kissed me, said not to worry, and oh by the way if I did evacuate, where would I be? Suddenly it occurred to me, where does one go when one lives on an island and all roads meander along the shoreline. Bill said if I tried to come to the landing, most likely it would be washed out at the seven-mile, cutting them off from us (they are above the eleven mile). I thought about this and told him I would probably (time allowing) go to the airport and head up the hills.

Then we realized that this would be happening within the next few hours and if anything did occur the results would be over long before he got home. So I said if the worst happened and somehow the boat wasn't here anymore, I would be at the bunkhouse, or where it used to be, by the time he got home. With that he kissed me and was off.

Not even relaxed, I sat in the boat, waiting.

At noon the VHF cackled to life, it was Ketchikan Coast Guard with the latest update. A one-foot wave had passed through Dutch Harbor. The *tsunami* warning was still very much in effect.

It was at this moment I thought perhaps if I wrote this down, maybe it would alleviate some of my fears. As my eyes were not necessary to type, I was able to look around. What I saw was by no means encouraging. While people came and went as normal, the police, troopers, rescue squads, and fire engines were also much in evidence, very much UN-normal.

As I sat keying, I watched the tide increase above its normal high. The time for this *tsunami* to reach us was earlier estimated between 1 and 2 PM. Should this be the case, already the ramp down from the road was barely an incline. The waterline was less than five feet from the road. Looking at the tide book, suddenly I am interrupted by the Coast Guard radio, "*13:38 update - "This is an actual* tsunami *warning message. ... A wave of less than one foot has passed through Dutch Harbor as anticipated. ... A tsunami warning is still in effect, ... damage is not expected in Alaskan waters. ..."* What a relief to know we have nothing to fear in terms of one-hundred-foot waves.

Continuing to search the tide book, I found where high tide for today was at 12:36 PM at eleven point one feet. Thursday and Friday, the normal tide is scheduled to be twelve feet. Though relieved but still a little nervous, I waited for further developments.

To my delight and then sudden fear, it wasn't long before further developments developed, when Bill came home.

This could only mean major panic, why else would Bill be home unless something horrible were about to happen! When he walked in it was very quiet, calmly, I asked him why he was home. Sitting down he said, just to hold my hand. How wonderful! He went on to say, it appeared the wave that hit Dutch Harbor was indeed less than a foot, specifically two and a half inches. He said he'd run into the cops along Port St. Nicholas, they were telling everyone they needed to evacuate three hundred feet above shoreline or at least a mile inland. The cop said they didn't expect anything, but it was necessary to tell everyone.

Quietly we sat there. Waiting.

The next Coast Guard warning came on, same info, they were not anticipating severe conditions in Alaskan waters. Whew. I asked Bill when our wave was expected, he said 2PM.

We continued to wait.

Suddenly Bill looked up pointing and said, "Here it comes!" My insides turned upside down as I turned around to face uncertain destiny. Seeing the foot wave push toward the dock, we both laughed a little shakily as we noticed it was the wake from a boat coming in.

Bill said Art, a pilot, and the crew were calling it the big salami. Turning on the helicopter radio we listened to them banty back and forth. One fellow asked if Art could see anything, he said no, but he was looking. Another said this was his first tidal wave and frankly he was a little disappointed. Art responded that he'd called Ketchikan weather and the *tsunami* had been delayed four hours, until the next high tide. Arkie, one of the 'hookers,' as the woods crew is called, came back and said Art was full of it. Then another fellow replied that Art was causing a tidal wave in his lake, the water he was hooking logs in, Art said he was only trying to help, one way or another.

By this time Bill had been home nearly an hour. While we were sitting there waiting, a fellow came and asked if Bill was a mechanic, he said yes and the fellow asked if he'd come listen to his engine, something was wrong. Bill said sure and left.

While he was gone, the *MISKITO* and *ZENETH* came in. Bill talked with them a few minutes to find they had gone out in the bay to ride the wave rather than be caught in the harbor and the possibility of being sucked dry. They said they hadn't seen anything so came back. When Bill came home, he repeated this and said he had to go. He helped me pack the laundry up to the van and went back to work.

Later when I was at the laundry I ran into Juliana, off the *LADY ALICE.* We shared stories and she told how Nick had seen her loading things up to their motorhome for evacuation. She laughed and said no, they were pulling out this weekend, it wasn't because of today. I told her I had seen her doing the same thing and it did not lend me any confidence, then to see her drive away and not come back added to my overload.

When I was done I raced home. To my relief the boat was still there. It didn't look like a *tsunami* had happened while I'd been away. Turning the VHF back on, it was in time to hear the Coast Guard break in for another update, *"...at 4:34 PM they had canceled the local* tsunami *warning. Be advised there could still be some tidal fluctuations but that nothing was expected."* End of warning. End of *tsunami* Tuesday.

Termination Dust is Imminent

November A Winding Down

Termination Dust, otherwise known as snow, usually signals the end of the logging season in Alaska. Altho we hadn't gotten any at sea level, the tops of the ridges glistened white in the morning sun.

Halloween was fun, we got seven trick-or-treaters, all kids from our crew. Bill carved us a pumpkin, something we hadn't done in years. Stuffing a flashlight in it, we displayed it proudly on the bow.

This will be the first Thanksgiving ever, that we don't do something for others. Usually I cook dinner for us and any strays, but here the fellows are being quite well fed at the bunkhouse. So instead, we decided to join them.

Laurel, the cook, is very nice. However, rather than have the traditional turkey, which Laural had cooked throughout the year, she decided to do the 'end of season dinner' of steak and lobster, gee, that's too bad.

At last Bart, now 'The Alaska Project Manager,' was convinced to see that we should take the ferry from Ketchikan through to Bellingham. Beau, Laurel's husband, had already left for Washington and said the roads in Canada were treacherous, with snow up to the edge of his hood. Bill told Bart, for us there was no question about going on the ferry, but he would battle for the remaining six others with vehicles. Boy am I relieved. It will only be thirty-six hours as opposed to four days. Although I am worried about Moldie, she gets so seasick.

Winter is trying desperately to get here. The harbor is littered with logs both big and little. Yesterday we had spitting snow mixed with thunder and lightning. The woos that I am made it very difficult to leave the security of the bunkhouse for a metal boat sitting in salt water. After Bill got home, he reminded me it was fiberglass. To be honest, it wouldn't have made any difference if it had been made of marshmallow.

One of the rare sunny days this month combined with Bill having an afternoon off, so we played log raft. Since the first storm in September logs had been collecting in the basin. As they came near the boat, Bill would tie them to the dock. Today we gathered them in bundles of three to five logs and towed them out to sea with the skiff. Despite the sun being out and it two in the afternoon, the temperature never got much above 30°.

Feeling the cold bite of the wind on our face was refreshing at first, but after about the third load I was frozen to the point I couldn't feel my fingers anymore. Besides, it was nearly three and the sun was setting brilliant pink on the surrounding snow-covered mountains.

Bribing Bill, I told him if this were our last load, I'd buy him a bottle of whiskey. When the last log was shoved off, he agreed wholeheartedly and away we went slicing through the dark, frigid waters.

Shortly after the beginning of the month, Bill and I were talking about the fact we hadn't seen Colby in almost two months and wondered where he was. Deciding to check a little further, I asked Nick, the Harbor Master, and he seemed to think he might still be up around Sitka.

As usual when one thinks of someone out of the blue, within a few days one hears something, literally. Soon one morning we heard Colby putta-putting into the harbor. On my way to take the garbage up I saw him sitting in the shade of a boat with his shirt off.

Looking down, not only was I wearing shoes, but socks, two layers and a coat, I demanded to know why he was trying to catch pneumonia in this less than 30° sunny AM! Turning slightly he said, 'see my back?' I had already noticed his arms had a diamond grid, obviously he had been burned severely at some time, but his back was a mess. He explained they had done skin grafts less than a year ago and the nerve endings should be dead, but weren't. He said the slightest sweat set him on fire, and yes, he knew he was lucky he didn't get sick.

Somewhat at a loss for words I asked lamely what had he been up to. In a few short sentences he summed up his past two months, saying he had ran into a bear that while he wasn't frightened, he was very much 'aware' and the gun he was packing didn't feel adequate; he'd attended a Halloween party where the winners were dressed like hot tubs; he was sorry they had torn down the public buildings around the hot springs; he'd managed to run aground 'in a channel fraught with hazards'; and he'd been late out of the water by a few minutes at the sea cucumber fishery, thus getting a ticket.

Appalled by his apparent run of bad luck, I told him I hoped November would be better and hurried off. The rest of the day I thought about those few sentences and wondered how and why to all of them. What was he doing on shore in the first place that he ran into the bear, where were these hot springs, did they really give tickets for being a few minutes late out of the water? Needless to say I let my imagination take over and wrote Colby his own story.

It took several days, and then I let Bill read it only to deflate me by saying it could easily offend Colby. Horrified I asked by what, there wasn't anything offensive there. He pointed out the reference to God, the emotions of each situation, all of it. Dejected I said I'd toss it. I had thought it was a good idea. Soothing my ruffled feathers he said no, but be aware of the potential.

Seeing Colby a few days later nervously I told him what I was doing and that Bill thought I might offend him. Smiling, he said I could never offend him and that he knew it wouldn't be intentional, if at all. Hesitantly I asked his point of view on God. Echoing the story line, he claimed he wasn't a Christian, but let me off the hook by saying his sister was. Relieved I told him he'd see the results in a few days.

Like a nervous ninny, I almost chickened out giving him the short story. After I did, several days went by before we saw each other again. Thanking me, he boosted my ego tremendously when he said it was good and that we'd be amazed if we knew how close to the truth it actually had been. Wishing him a happy holiday, that was the last time we saw him as he left for another fishery the next day.

Colby's story follows this one, titled '*Adventures of the F/V KOLH*'

Un-launching of *M/V ROTORWASH*, or 'Moving Day' Sunday - November 20

When I climbed out of the V-berth at 7:30 AM, Sunnahae and the mountains around Port St. Nick were all visible and the sky was clear to at least 3,000'. It looked like the sunrise was going to be especially pretty all bright whites and golds.

By the time Bill climbed out at 9AM and went for his attitude adjustment, the sky had lowered, Sunnahae was clagged, and it was beginning to gently spit snow. (Before he got to the restroom he saw a notice on the Harbor Masters door and wondered if it read that the facilities were closed for the winter! They weren't)

Ah yes, Moving Day.

High tide was at 1PM, but looking at the thickening snow we figured we'd give it a try sooner. We failed to check the precise time we got under way, but at last check, it was 12:15 PM. We were supposed to go get Keaton, but Jake showed up so we cast off with him as crew instead.

Ole and Sven were their usual uncooperative selves. It took quite a bit of effort before they finally caught and then began to grudgingly cooperate with each other. It had something to do with lack of choke. As soon as Bill had started fiddling with the engines Moldie dove for cover. Sweetpea, our biggest kittie was already down under, and Stinkpot curled up between them on top of the blankets.

Visibility by now was poor on the mountains, but still fair on the water. The snow hadn't let up any but the wind was light and seas pretty mellow, considering. Pulling into the docks on the north side the wind was blowing harder. Fortunately it was a head wind, so all Bill had to do was fight the forward situation and center on the trailer. I in my might, stayed on the dock and took pictures.

Jake stood on the trailer giving Bill signals which way to steer. It took a few tries but soon *ROTORWASH* was settled. As Jake began inching up the ramp the snow storm hit seriously. (*Thank you Lord for waiting on us!*) Within the few minutes it took to top out the ramp, tie the boat secure, and get to our respective vehicles, it dropped enough to cover the ground, wet and all, and began stacking up. By the time we were underway it was at least a half inch!

Bill crept his way up the hill, Jake right behind should the boat give way. It took a while to get the van going. So by the time I got to the bunkhouse Bill was trying to get the boat backed in next to it. After a few tries here too, soon we were level. Unfortunately, there was no way to get on the boat. The only ladder available looked a bit rickety and I commented on it. Bill replied dryly that that was an understatement! Not only was the top step missing, there were no stringers to hold it together. Surprisingly, when I tried it, it felt rather secure to me, but Bill wasn't happy.

Jumping in the truck, we took a drive to the service landing for a better ladder. It was so beautiful up there, fresh snow everywhere. We visited with Hank long enough to find out that Oak Ridge, Oregon, about 2500' elevation had over ten inches of snow at present (*UGH!*). While we were there, I scared myself when I walked up around the corner to 'visit nature' and came across a fresh set of bear tracks.

Bill set up the ladder while I began scrapping on the hull. The four and a half months with little attention provided us with a VERY healthy assorted and sundry plant selection. At least I think those things were plants. Although there were a variety of truly gross blobs too. At least the colors were pretty, purple, dark red, bright orange, crystal clear.

When I was finally able to get aboard, the new ladder was almost worse than the old. It set a bit away from the hull, was tall and narrow, and took both hands as well as crawling on your knees to get in. With the temp hanging in the low 30°s and the freezing rain, it could prove to be quite challenging. As I walked in, I was delighted to see that the kitties had not become sea sick. I hadn't fed them well for breakfast so they were quite pleased to see me.

We didn't have electricity, so Bill ran a cord through the window of the cookhouse but the box only allowed one thing to be plugged in. Luckily it was the heater. We had 12 volt, but that makes for dim lighting.

Rumor has the job finished in two days, then do a short forty-some turn cleanup across the lake. That puts things done on the 23rd. It is unfortunate for those who might wish to get home for Thanksgiving, but ... The other crew expects to finish the 26th or so. I wouldn't be surprised if we didn't jump over to their job and help. As it stands, we are all booked off the island and out the 30th, although Bill and I leave Prince of Wales the evening of the 29th.

As an aside, Bill picked up the weekend paper. In one section is a little game that spells a message, depending on how many letters in one's name, add four. Bill is number seven and I'm six. He did mine and it said to 'Act on ideas.' I told him I had a great idea, rather than me cook dinner, let's go get pizza, and we acted on it.

A New Family Member Monday - November 21

Typically of most evenings, one will find me sitting in front of the keyboard (tho *sitting* anywhere in the boat is limited), so when Bill climbed in the cabin I looked up and smiled Hi. He returned the smile and said 'Hi Grams.' Puzzled, 'Grams,' I said, then 'GRAMS! We had a grand baby! What was it! When! What's its name?!'

Holding his hands up as if to physically block the barrage of questions, he shook his head and said, 'All I know is it's a boy.' Laughing he said he'd gotten a note to call Jack, 'would I like to go up to Keaton's room to find out more?' Nearly plowing over him, out the door we went.

Calling Astoria we chatted with our son Willie and his young lady Krysti. Justin Mitchell Kyle was born Monday, November 7, 1994. Willie was proud, Krysti was sore, and the baby was just fine. They had trouble getting thru to us so had finally called Jack for help.

They wanted to know when we might be down. We told them we'd be leaving in a few days but would try to get there as soon as possible. Wishing them God's best and lots of love, we rung off.

With a warm glow we were very proud of our son and even more proud we had a new grandson! With a little tingle we wondered how his arrival would affect our world.

Termination Dust Wins! or More Commonly Known As 'Shut Down'
Saturday - November 26

At first, Bill had thought we were going to move over to Hollis this date and live on the boat in the parking lot until time to catch the ferry three days later. Instead, after spending two days of running back and forth moving all the equipment he said it would be okay for us to go over Monday.

(An extra set of trips was made because a fellow from the barge line had said it would be okay to park the two loaders *(116,000 pounds each!)*, fuel truck, service vans, and fifteen trucks along their road because they wouldn't have a barge in until Tuesday. Then late Saturday night they tracked Bill down to say he had to move everything because someone forgot they had a barge coming in Sunday!!)

When Bill left about 9AM to convoy trucks, I braced up in foul weather gear to finish scraping most of the crud off the bottom of the hull. The wind was slashing the sleet and the wind-chill was probably around 15°. When Bill came over to kiss me see-you-later, he pointed at the small area I had scraped clean, but not polished. He told me I had to get it down to bare, white-shiny hull, or when we landed in Seattle they would quarantine the boat and require we get a health certificate. Frowning, dismayed, already chilled, and astounded they'd require such a thing, I settled in for a *very* long job requiring far too much elbow grease.

Around 3PM I was so frozen I couldn't have scraped another barnacle had there been one. Although the hull was smooth (a much better job than I had expected to do), it wasn't polished except for a small area about three feet square. Figuring I would take a quick break to get some hot tea, lunch, and thaw out a little, Bill pulled in from another trip to Hollis.

When he saw how wet and stiff my hair was, he asked in disbelief 'What are you doing out here?!' I told him there was no way we were going to get quarantined if I could help it and I was polishing the hull like he had said to do! What did he think I was out there for, a suntan?!

Now I have always admired my husband for his brains and truly have wished to be as smart as he. However, this day, he made perhaps a tiny little error in judgment. Laughing and shaking his head, he meekly replied, 'I was only kidding, there's no such thing as a health certificate for the hull of a boat!'

I am here to tell you with icy water dripping off my nose, unfeeling feet in sleet-soaked shoes, and fingers numb to the bone, my husband is alive and well today because of these very facts. A tourist may well have thought the northern lights were out dancing so early in the day from the pretty blue haze crackling around.

But we know the truth, don't we.

Southbound

Departures
Monday - November 28; Ketchikan, Alaska

Ah yes, yet *another* moving day.

This morning Bill and several other fellows went over to Hollis about 7AM with the last load. Although Sunday night was only rain in Craig, across the little hill that everyone calls a pass (maybe 500') it had snowed and was frozen. From the stories everyone told it was pretty slick.

When Bill got back we finished packing-out. He hooked the boat to Hank's truck, the kitties and I were in the van, and Jake hooked up his trailer. At last we were away.

The road up to the bottom of the pass was wet but clear. It was snowing pretty hard but not sticking yet. Going up the pass, the road became slush and by the top Bill was creeping and the tracks indicated he had a few wheels that were spinning. Once on top, he pulled us all over and chained the truck and van, while Jake did his truck and trailer. Unfortunately, there were no chains for the boat trailer.

While we chained up, Hank with his camper and a mechanic from the other crew passed us, creeping along also. When we got back in the car and underway, I asked Bill if I needed to be scared, he said no. So I asked why did he chain me? He replied if he'd chained his truck and not me, he'd never hear the end of it.

True.

Going down the other side was v-e-r-y s-l-o-w, but the road wasn't all that bad. In fact, at the bottom by Harris River it had cleared again with a few patches of packed snow. The rest of the way in, except for Maybeso Creek, was relatively clear. Although by now the snow had stepped it up and became huge snowflakes about the size of tangerines.

We had been running on bare pavement for over five miles and I was feeling a little guilty because I knew how much Bill hated driving with chains. That is, until we rounded one corner and a truck was flipped upside down in a ditch. They had been extremely lucky because the cab wasn't damaged at all as it fit perfectly in the ditch. Suddenly, I was very glad for those chains even though the road was clear.

Hollis wasn't plowed, but then it was only about three inches deep. We all pulled in and made ourselves cozy. Bill had made sure *Mr. Heater* was in the van so the kitties would stay warm. We all sat there for the next several hours visiting. Noting the time, we had left the bunkhouse at 1:30 PM and arrived thirty-eight miles later at 3PM.

Finally the ferry came in. They began loading about 6:30 PM and let Bill on about 7PM. Lanes one through three went on and then it was my turn. All this time, Sweetpea had been under the blankets, but Moldie was on top of them and Stinkpot was quietly snuggled on my lap.

After we got parked and the kitties settled, we went up to the forward Observation Lounge. Looking around the room, I was surprised to discover there were only about five people I didn't know. Pulling out of Hollis the weather was wet snow, but calm. When we hit Clarence Strait the wind picked up and the waves were such that we did a fair amount of pitching and tossing.

Pulling into Ketchikan we didn't have anything to be concerned about, the roads were bare but wet. While everyone off-loaded, Bill went into the terminal to ask if we could park all the rigs back by the fence. They said no problem. Reservations had been made at the Best Western across the street. Jake checked us in and fortunately we were able to take the kitties in too. Moldie had been wonderful and no one had gotten seasick!

After we got back to The Landing and tucked ourselves in Bill had a welcome glass of whiskey and wanted to talk. By 2AM I was falling asleep and told him we needed to call it a night, as he had to be up by 8 AM the next morning.

The next day Bill spent running around Ketchikan getting everything tucked in for the winter, for when we'd return in the spring. I played tourist and did some early Christmas shopping.

The phone rang as Bill was getting out of bed. He had set the alarm, or so we thought. Bart was on the phone wanting to know where he was, it was almost 9AM! Of course he immediately got testy. A quick shower and he was off.

I wasn't sure what to do with myself so leisurely got up and went down and had a cup of tea with toast. A few hours later I went back and had a cup of tea and a bowl of soup. Finally I saw Bill for a few minutes and he said he'd be gone for three or four more hours. So again I was on my own. Deciding I didn't want to just sit in the room I grabbed the shuttle and went downtown for some early Christmas shopping.

Already dusky by 3PM, I was dismayed I still had about two miles to walk. It was also getting cold and beginning to spit snow. Stopping in Silver Lining I checked to see if they had any sea cucumbers. They did, a mere $12.75 per pound.

By the time I stopped at the bookstore, then at the liquor store for Bill another bottle of whiskey, it was snowing harder and really cold. I was very happy to get back to the motel. Bill had gotten home ahead of me and already had had a long hot bath.

After dinner in the motel restaurant, we retired to our room for an early night.

Wednesday, to our shock, we awoke to over eight inches of snow! Minutes before noon checkout we raced around, threw our gear together, and packed the kitties out to the van. By the time we got to the ferry landing, a little over a hundred feet, it was snowing again and would get much harder as the day went on.

The ferry had asked that we sweep all the snow off the vehicles. That took several hours, but finally we were done and loaded. Everyone was on and we were all tucked into our individual staterooms. Hank was sharing one with us, but the room didn't turn out to be all that bad. Twin bunk beds, but a huge shower.

When we finally got underway, 4:38 PM it was dark and a blizzard was blowing. The announcement by the Captain of the *M/V MALASPINA* said it could turn quite nasty in three different locations: Dixon Entrance about two hours south, Chatham Sound at Milbank around 6AM, and then Queen Charlotte Sound between 11AM and 1PM. He went on to say there was a big storm brewing, so to expect severe seas.

The first thing that caused a bit of concern wasn't more than ten miles south of Ketchikan. It was very dark, but with all the snow and lights reflecting from town, we could see the huge clumps of snow clinging to all the trees on the west side of Pennock Island. Then they shone the light over the water and it was a forest in the waterway, there were logs and other natural debris everywhere! It was a little disconcerting to see all the snow heaped on them too! It looked like a bunch of mini-icebergs.

We sat in the forward lounge or observation deck. There was a group of Elderhostel on the boat and a film of the karst systems of Southeast including Prince of Wales was being shown, so Bill and I enjoyed a last look at El Capitan and Prince of Wales. An interesting note, Prince of Wales and Southeast is one of the few location where muskeg sits directly on top of the karst. Muskeg is wetlands or bogs, usually between three feet and nine feet deep. It's made up of water and decomposing vegetation. Walking on it can be dangerous because it can grow over the top of water. In this case, the acid runoff from the muskegs can have an immediate impact on the karst, which is soluble rock like limestone or gypsum, and can create sinkholes or hollowing to make caves.

Dinner was at 6PM, exactly as we entered Dixon Entrance. (I wondered if timing was such to keep food costs down. Interesting theory.) Jake felt we had twelve-foot seas, some upwards of twenty foot.

In no time we had passed out of the entrance and by 9PM the first car deck announcement was made. Bill and I went down to check on the kitties. They hadn't fared as well as I, but we could only find two spots to clean up. Moldie was looking like her namesake and Stinkpot wasn't happy, but Sweetpea seemed cozy under the wool blanket.

That evening Bill wanted a drink, so soon we met Hank in the bar. Although the fellows drank stronger fair, I stuck to *Seven-up*. Conversation came and went, but a statement Hank made struck me as funny, 'He (Hank) is never lost, he just sometimes doesn't know where the rest of the world is in relation to him.' I can relate to that.

International waters south of Bella Bella, British Columbia
Thursday, December 1

Although it was overcast and still snowing, the waves and breakers had a certain beauty to them.

Hank was up and awake by 4AM, but Bill and I lazed about for another couple of hours. Then suddenly, Bill who never gets up before noon on his day off decided he wanted a cup of coffee at 6:30 AM!! I wanted to stay put but within a few minutes the first roll of Milbank Sound hit and I decided if I wanted a shower I had better get it done before the corkscrewing of the ship was too much.

The shower felt pretty good, but the ceiling was taller than I was accustomed to so when we rolled, I didn't have my normal steadier. Catching up with the boys in the dining room, they had finished their morning *tete-a'-tete*.

The water had smoothed out by then (it was a short crossing) and tho it was overcast and still snowing the waves and breakers had a certain beauty to them.

While checking out our progress, I noticed a clean-cut fellow looking thru a very small box. Turns out it was one of the new Camcorders, 8 MM, but only a little bigger than a book. I had seen the commercial on TV the day before in Ketchikan. Nosy me I asked how much and he said it was $800, the cheapest one available. I decided next year we would return with one.

Conversing with the fellow, we found out after five years at Elmendorf Air Force Base in Anchorage he was being transferred to Okinawa. He was en route this minute to Colorado. He swore he saw an Orca but we think he probably saw a Dall's porpoise, which has the same coloring and is often thought to be a baby Orca.

As with most ferry rides, this one had a group of Elderhostel. Throughout the day we attended their various lectures.

The first Elderhostel lecture we attended was called Shake and Swirl, about *tsunami's* and other natural phenomenon's. Some of the new theories immerging are that glaciers are fluctuating because of a natural greenhouse effect (too much carbon dioxide, CO_2, in the atmosphere). This is based on a paper written in Sweden. It says something to the effect plants digest the atmospheric CO_2 and return the oxygen. I didn't know what this meant, but it sounded interesting, maybe.

Thru a fluke, they discovered the Japanese Current that brings warm water up to the Arctic from Japan, then splits at the Aleutians and drifts south along Southeast, doesn't.

In 1990 there was a sneaker spill, several crates of *Nikes* fell off a container barge. Eventually the box split up and the sneakers sailed away. When they started landing on shore, quite some time later, they traced back to this spill. (Much later there was a sneaker swap of the stranded singles through ads in the newspaper!)

However, in 1992 rubber duckies and other tub toys, 29,000 to be exact, were released and tracked. Four-hundred plus were found north of Chichagof Island and a lot came ashore near Sitka. At this time the current then came straight in from Siberia to the Southeast coastline. Taking wind data from the past several El Nino's they have found there is different circulation during different years. (By the way, it took a couple of years for the duckies to come in and they also found they were pretty resilient, the plastic didn't show any signs of deterioration.)

Even as far south as we were and by 9AM it was still snowing relatively hard, but the shoreline showed that it wasn't at sea level, but several hundred feet up. The previous evening we had heard that between Prince Rupert and somewhere farther south, maybe about 100 Mile House, the Canadian roads were closed during the night and cars were only able to run daylight hours. Can you imagine what that would be like for those on our crew who like to run twenty-four hours a day?

A particularly enjoyable lecture was on 'Living in Southeast, Alaska.' It filled us with all kinds of facts and figures we seem to so enjoy spouting.

For example, according to the women lecturer 'we have adapted to our environment'. Such as residents of Hyder, Alaska use Canadian currency, except Forest Service personnel (she didn't explain why they didn't). She then went on to describe some of the differences between Southeast living and Outside, (Outside to always be spelled with a capitol O) and referring to the Lower-48 (also always capitalized) or the 48-Continental United States.

Working was her first topic. Obviously fishing, logging, and tourism were the main employers. Some noted differences was the mode of transportation for the logs. Logging needs barges. To fish with a crew required a permit, of which Alaska has over 35,000, and not surprisingly 80% of the tourist come in summer. Seasons affect all types of work, with lots of entrepreneurship, like the army of trucks with snowplows in Juneau.

She went on to describe the various recreation opportunities living in the archipelago affords, and managed a complete sideline on 'Southeast slippers,' or rain boots to the Outside world.

As we were passing a tug with barge in tow, transportation was the next topic. People ooh'ed and well'ed when it was pointed out that *everything* comes to Southeast that way, from food and milk, to lumber and poinsettias, etc.

Surprisingly not everyone realized air transportation dominated or how vital small planes were to the communities. The ferry, or Alaska Marine Highway, is state owned and a lifeline to Southeast. Obviously when planes can't fly, the ferry may be the only available mode of travel.

In 1992 over 400,000 passengers and over 100,000 vehicles were transported via ferry. Only thick dense fog, usually near Wrangell, and winds around Skagway are the few things that stop them.

Schooling brought quite a discussion. Unfortunately, the attitude was more disgruntled than applauding at the innovative ways Southeast had created to be a part of the surrounding land masses. In competition such as debating or basketball, traveling is most often by ferry, altho some basketball teams fly. A buzz was heard round the lounge when it was mentioned some school days were missed to do this.

Based on Juneau Douglas High School, $240,000 was spent in 1992 on transportation for activities. However it didn't come out of the budget. According to the lecturer, if you are a coach you need to be a good fund raiser! Apparently, it has been found that Southeast has a stronger bond among school kids because of being away from home and staying in each other's homes overnight.

There is only one football team in Southeast, they are from Juneau. They play against Seattle, Anchorage, Fairbanks, and somewhere in British Columbia. Juneau has a football holiday tournament, and each team pays between $1500-2000 just to play. Of course they fly to get where they are going but they have to raise the funds to do so.

Not surprisingly Home School is a common event. The Southeast program was distinguished because it was a geographical need. Some lessons are received thru RATNET - Rural Alaska Television Network TV. This company has a package deal from all stations, ABC, NBC, CBS, TNN, CNN, CMT, etc. And if one has a telephone, they can do Independent Study over it for an hour, for two or three days a week.

While the lecturer addressed Health Care, Bill and I didn't necessarily agree with her assessment. She was accurate when she stated it was always a concern. Apparently Juneau is considered the hub for medical care in northern Southeast and Ketchikan for southern. She said both locations have fairly well-developed hospitals, with Sitka, Petersburg, and Wrangell having outreach hospitals. We didn't realize fund raisers were held for the EM's because they don't have any funding.

When retirement was brought up we wanted to laugh, knowing my sisters situation, as in no retirement funds other than Social Security. The lecturer was truthful when she said it was "different in Alaska". Unfortunately recent changes had cut lots of programs that were State devised to keep seniors in the state as a natural resource. For instance, the Pioneers home in Sitka, that was built in 1917 to help loggers and miners in early days. Others are in Juneau, Ketchikan, and the Interior (meaning not Southeast). Used to, one had to be in the state for fifteen years to receive a longevity bonus, a monthly fund to seniors over sixty-five. Now, only one year residency is required. This year the stipend was $200, but in 1997 it ends.

The next general topic was everyday living conditions, things most people take for granted, such as garbage. She immediately got everyone's attention when she asked in general if they kept a lid on their cans to keep the dogs out?, well for us it was the bears! In Skagway community cleanup is trying to get rid of old cars. The only way available is to barge out the scrap metal to Outside for recycling. Recycling is still difficult because it's so expensive. In Juneau tho, one can recycle aluminum cans and white paper, and glass is being ground and used in road fill.

As we sat and looked around the room of fifty-odd people, all nearing sixty or older, we knew they didn't have a clue what she was talking about. When she commented on the roadside recycling bins in everyone's neighborhood, which I couldn't relate to, everyone nodded yes, they had them. I wondered what they were. But we knew they didn't fully grasp the idea of bears rummaging through garbage cans and raiding fish shacks where salmon is hung to dry. Or, the physical limitations of where to store wrecked or abandoned junk cars. Southeast simply had very few recycling facilities.

We were surprised when power brought on such a discussion. Of course we knew that diesel generators were the big deal in keeping villages and communities in electricity. Also all had supplemental power if only water by tapping lakes high in the mountains with turbines to generate power. A Hydropower dam was built in Juneau in the 1920's and Sitka has two dams. When Good Morning America came to Southeast, they were warned to bring their own generators. Hyder is the only community with outside power generation and it comes from Canada. Ketchikan too has a dam. Altho currently Prince of Wales is all by diesel, soon the hydro plant up on Black Bear Lake would be finished.

The discussion came from the adjustment on the fuel bill. For example, we knew from experience, Craig and Klawock both get a subsidy from the State. In our case, in the motorhome it made the difference between a $119 electric bill to $65 out of pocket. (Craig cents per kilowatt were .14 and Klawock was .42. How does this compare to what you pay?) It was mentioned Florida gets coal from Africa and New York gets some kind of adjustment also.

An interruption from the bridge clarified the current dip and buck, '...Fitzhugh Sound, swells from Hakai Passage about one mile east, ...' the lecturer was surprised and said they usually didn't feel the motion this far away.

Continuing the lecture, a shocking bit of news was that there was only six-percent private land in the state of Alaska! (I can only hope this was a misquote of figures) and between the Park and Forest Service, ninety-four percent is managed by the federal government! Back in 1979 a state lottery of land was set up, such as a $20 lottery ticket could net the winner a five-acre parcel of land. Of course it currently is on hold as it seems like everything in Alaska ends up in court.

Again it was no surprise as soon as dividend money was mentioned everyone was ready to move to Alaska. I had always wondered how the dividend came to be and was glad to learn. Seems every Alaskan is a shareholder in the state. Somehow twenty-five percent of all leases (on what I don't know) go into a trust fund for the residents. Each year they invest the funds in a variety of things and inflation proof that fund. After inflation, a dividend check is distributed to every resident, anywhere from $850 to over $1000. It was started by then governor Jay Hammond.

Around dividend time everything from hot tubs to tractors go on sale. Alaska Airlines had a deal, if the resident will turn over their dividend they receive four airline tickets anywhere Alaska goes. This year Mark Air entered the competition with up to five tickets and Northwest Airlines offered three.

Altho the money is 'free', there are some rules. One must be a resident for one year, and then can only be gone from the state a percentage of each year thereafter.

Food gathering came next, which of course meant salmon fishing to everyone. Many were surprised to find it is a lot more involved than that and food gathering affected almost everyone in Southeast. Obviously one way is hunting and fishing.

On Prince Of Wales alone, five deer were allowed each year. Subsistence is broadly translated as 'traditional and customary'. Altho now in the courts, it was still being defined, and they had discovered it to be a very complicated distinction but with priority over every other type, be it sport or commercial (hunting or fishing). However, there is no distinction between natives or non-natives except between marine mammals, i.e. seals. Personal Use came to be after subsistence laws, it was one way for urban people to get fish and aquatic plants. Personal Use has the last rights and one needs a fishing license and permit, and must use a dip net not fishing rod. Personally, I'm still confused.

A comment aside, there were more Hamm radio operators in the state than in the entire union and more privately owned aircraft per capita.

We were surprised it took so long to get around to talking about wages. The lecturer admitted she received a federal government twenty-five percent Cost Of Living Allowance to help compensate for the high cost of living. Tho she commented, they were still the lowest paid outfit in the state. She went on to add that seasonal employment, such as tour jobs usually were paid $5 per hour Outside, but here $8. The group was unwilling to believe that wages weren't higher. Bill dryly stated that it was minimum wage in most cases, but people gawffed at the idea.

The lady went on to explain that cannery workers didn't get paid hardly anything for working on the slime line. That the only reason they made money was because of the fifteen-hour days. In fact there was literally a limit set here for only twenty hours per day. And while housing is always at a premium in Southeast, in Petersburg there is a huge tent city in the summer because there is no place to live. (Case in point is us bringing a boat to live on.) She described how it wasn't uncommon for the locals to feel hostile, comparing the snow-birds to carpet baggers for not living here. Then told how Alaskans feel their natural resources have been exploited. I sat there, knowing we were those very same 'carpet baggers' and <u>knowing</u> that the Native corporation Columbia contracts with was definitely exploiting the timber industry and felt very small and almost dirty. I was grateful the folk of Craig and Klawock liked us personally.

The end of the lecture was a too brief couple of sentences describing the weather and how several feet of rain were endured (not uncommon to have 140+ inches!). Then she laughed and closed by telling us how Santa comes by ferry or float plane.

Not wanting to expose us for the cheats we were, I felt compelled to have to put in a plug for the helicopter logging industry. Knowing she was busy, I just briefly (can you believe that) described the job and purpose and told her she should look into it because not only is it the way of the future, i.e. enviro-safe, but very interesting.

As the lecture was ending, the Captain came on the loud speaker from the bridge and pointed out an island off our port. Apparently, *tsunamis* had wiped out Egg Island twice in the past many years, so all the main buildings have been moved to the other end of the island. Then he went on to say, 'our length is 408' with a 75' beam, currently the ground swells are also 400+' so walking is a hazard and *not* recommended. Please have a nice day.'

Soon the Captain was telling us that George Vancouver had aptly named this area over 200 years ago, Cape Caution. Watching beyond the boat, some of the breakers among the islands were quite spectacular. By 1:22 PM, the sun disappeared and the weather had turned back to poop with freezing rain driving into the decks and wind driven waves white capping about.

Watching a boat abreast of us about eighty-plus feet, it was not comforting to see him disappear from sight time and again. Jake said we turned more into the wind, and we could see waves come over the bow. Then the captain came on to say we had to tack sharply port, behind the fishing boat abeam of us, 'not to worry it is called storm tactics. Furthermore for a short time span we will be in the trough between swells, so please don't venture from your seats. Again have a nice day.'

Of course jokes ran rampant. Giles said we were changing positions to ram the other boat. The lecturer said for every turn we made; it kept us longer in the Queen Charlottes (oh by the way the lunch room was closed until further notice, I wonder why?!) Another women spoke up and said that at least they didn't charge for the extra time. Everyone laughed and talked about the line of seagulls following the boat. Jake said we didn't have seagulls we had sharks. (Chyum, chyum!)

Somewhere around 3PM the Captain came back on to say he had talked with Bellingham and there was only one cloud in the sky. Watching the driving sleet I looked over at Giles and told him when we got there, there was going to be two full days of nothing but sunshine. It never occurred to us that one cloud could take up the entire sky.

By evening we were ready to enter Seaborne Narrows which must be taken in slack tide. Bill and Hank had decided they were ready to imbibe in the bar. Not feeling up to anything of the sort I told Bill I'd find a cozy spot to work on the computer. Soon the dinner bell had rang. Because of still high seas there was a noticeable lack of diners.

The meal the evening before had been quite nice, if a little spendy. This night was pork chops with peas. Making a disgusted face I told the waiter no peas please. Quite pleasantly, he asked if I'd rather have a piece of squash. Delighted, I thanked him for being so accommodating. Salad was just iceberg lettuce. This was fresher than anything we could get on the Island. On of our first stops was usually at a buffet where we'd pig out on salads!

Too soon dinner was done and the long evening loomed ahead of us. Darkness had fallen well before 4:30 PM and the ferry didn't run with lights on in either lounge or forward observation deck, so cards, reading or the computer was out. Bored, we wandered to the forward deck. A set of charts were set up from one of the earlier lectures so Bill used his flashlight and we checked our progress to find we were about six hours north of Campbell River, British Columbia, on the east side of Vancouver Island. Running to the Pursuers Office every few hours I kept an official check of our location and progress.

On one such visit I found the spec sheet on the *M/V MALASPINA*:

M/V MALASPINA

OWNER - State of Alaska

DESIGNER - Phillip F. Spaulding & Associates

BUILDER - Puget Sound Bridge & Dry Dock Co.

Seattle, Washington

PRICE - $4.7 Million

Keel Laid - 01-05-62 Launched - 06-04-62

Contract Delivery - 08-03-62 Actual Delivery 01-21-63

Stretched 50' - 1972

Dimensions

Length overall, molded 408'

Draft design load 15'

Full displacement at design 3,585 tons

Service speed 18 kts

load draft (salt water); designed load draft

Vertical clearance, car deck 14'

Rudders 2

Propellers(2 -4 blades each.) 10' 6" diameter

Shaft rpm maximum controllable pitch 200

Bow thrusters 600 hsp

Horse power maximum (new 1972) 8,000

Propulsion

Two 4061 B.H.P. 4 cycle turbo charged enterprise diesels

Non-reversing type dmrv 12/3. Reduction gears, 1.88:1 ratio with 200 rpm output.

Power Generation

Three 3508, 800 hsp, 560 kW, caterpillar generators.

Fuel consumption at 800 hsp is 42 gallons/hour.

Generators were installed in Portland, Oregon 1989.

Capacities

Fuel oil diesel 125,000 gal

Clean lube oil 3,000 gal

Fresh water 105,250 gal

Burns fuel per hour 320 gal
Burns fuel per minute 5 gal
Vehicles 120
Maximum vans 21
Accommodations
Passengers 701 Staterooms 86 Berthing 274
Dining Room 150 Bar 84
Average run time - average cruise speed is 16.5 knots (approx 19 miles per hour)
Route Hours Miles
Bellingham - Ketchikan 36 570
Juneau - Haines 4.3 77.6
Prince Rupert - Ketchikan 6 105.8
Haines - Skagway 1 14.4
Ketchikan - Wrangell 5.5 99.7
Sitka - Petersburg 10 176
Wrangell - Petersburg 3 46
Sitka - Juneau 8.3 151.8
Petersburg - Juneau 7.8 122.2

Big deal, who cares.

Well, Bill did.

When we found Hank forward, sitting in the front row with a huge window on a sea of black nothingness. Joining him, soon we were solving the problems of the world. When the lights of Campbell River, British Columbia, started sliding by, I asked Bill what time it was, image our shock to find it almost 2 AM!

After passing the large community rather than the lights beginning to diminish, they actually started increasing as we neared the more populous Victoria, Vancouver and anticipated Bellingham. All along this water course we could see the small dotted lights of the different collections of towns, communities and other gatherings. Yawning goodnight, Hank gave us time to get tucked in bed while he took a quick smoke. Setting the alarm it was a matter of hours before we would all be headed 'home'.

Near Bellingham, Washington
Friday - December 2

Despite less than three hours of sleep, Hank was again up and out by 4:30 AM Friday morning. Bill soon followed, which of course required my oozing out of that warm comfy bed. Making a hasty check of the room and packing the last of the toiletries, I found both fellows leaning on the rails watching the lights of Bellingham come into view. Still too early to see, we wondered what the weather was like. All we could tell was that it wasn't driving rain.

After a light breakfast, we found the day had begun to break and we were delighted to see an almost clear sky.

By 7:30 AM we had docked at Bellingham and the call to our cars was made. We were surprised to learn that we could have landed in Bellingham hours earlier and even off-loaded, but because of the union, the dock workers refused to start any earlier than 8AM. What a sour piece of news this was.

It was nearly 9AM before we were off loaded and fueled ready to hit I-5 south. Watching the traffic zip past I could feel myself tightening with tension. It had been months since I'd driven faster than 35 mph!

Bill gave the thumbs up, grimacing I returned it.

The morning rush was well over by the time we got to Sedro Wooley, but a new hazard had developed. One look at the lowered, sleet-colored skies with rain and I sent heavenward a silent 'no, please.' The first snow flake fell anyway.

A mile can make all the difference and in no time we were flying along on a snow-frozen road. Reducing speed as quickly as possible, I tried to control the van from sliding.

Fighting tears and the van, I watched in horror as a bus and I came together like two magnets in slow motion. At what seemed like the last possible second, the bus broke traction and I surged ahead. Bill came back on the CB radio and said he would find a place for us to get off the freeway as soon as possible.

Before he had hardly finished the words, we drove out of it. Just like that it was gone.

Not long after 11AM we pulled into Seattle. Bill was hungry and I had more urgent needs. The sun had come out and was blindingly bright, but with so many air holes in the van I was frozen stiff. Later in the afternoon, with exhausted sighs we both pulled safely into Brooks.

The past eight months had been long but happy. Living on a boat was a wonderful new experience and it gave us lots of incredible memories. However, we couldn't deny it was so very good to see our loved ones and in our case always remember 'home is where the heart is'.

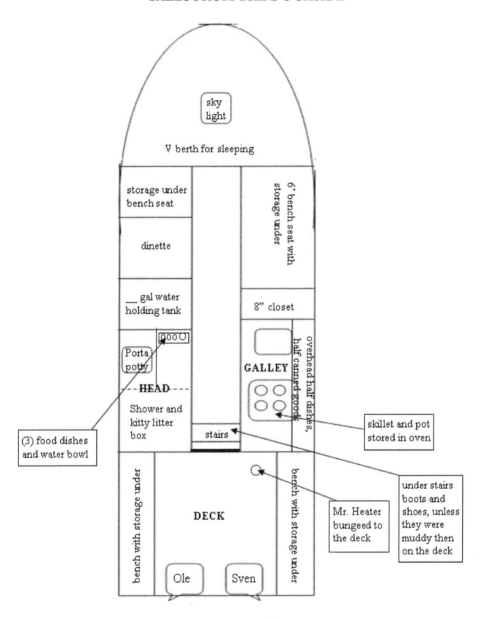

sky light

V berth for sleeping

storage under bench seat

dinette

6' bench seat with storage under

___ gal water holding tank

8" closet

Porta potty

overhead half dishes, half canned goods

GALLEY

- - HEAD - - -

Shower and kitty litter box

stairs

(3) food dishes and water bowl

skillet and pot stored in oven

bench with storage under

DECK

Mr. Heater bungeed to the deck

bench with storage under

under stairs boots and shoes, unless they were muddy then on the deck

Ole

Sven

1973 Bertram Flybridge 28' Cruiser*

*Picture is not to scale.

We May Have Stayed In Alaska Too Long - IF

by Levinia and Hank
Night watch

1. There is ice on the rotor blades.

2. The Submarina - Ice Cream Shop closes.

3. Bill Kyle's front yard freezes over.

4. Ozzie buys snowshoes for the hookers.

5. The stove in the van starts using more Jet-A than '74'.

6. The big, black bears begin to hibernate.

7. Chuck & Doug install ice cleats and bear claw chains on the loaders.

8. Keaton starts wearing a hat.

9. Jake buys a 4x4 equipped with a snowplow.

10. Ozzie plans a company Christmas party at the Fireweed lodge.

11. Giles stores his boat and starts fishing in an ice shanty.

12. Arkie builds on a wanigan for his growing family.

13. Santa isn't the <u>only</u> one using a sleigh for his sole method of transportation.

14. There are little, green Christmas trees and reindeer decorating the chow hall.

15. Art trades his blue windbreaker in on a parka.

16. We find ourselves cashing our checks for our Christmas Profit Sharing at NBA.

17. You can hear the "call of the geese" and you think they are saying, 'Head south! Head south!'.

18. Jan knits sweaters and mittens for their 'Three Little Kittens'.

19. Giles starts planning to marry locally to obtain better deer hunting privileges.

20. Jet Ranger Rick reports that air traffic includes a sleigh pulled by reindeer.

21. Bart is trying to decide whether he should trade his work-boat for a snowmobile or a dog-sled.

22. The people on POW think of us as part of the local population.

And; perhaps, the most obvious of all, they end Daylight Savings Time; because there is no more daylight to save!!!

23. (Added by Giles) You have enough time to think of a list of "You Know You've Been in Alaska Too Long When ...!"

24. (Added by Bill) The moss that was growing in the window tracks on the boat, is higher than the edge and showing signs of more vigorous growth.

BAD BOAT DAY!

You know it's going to be a bad day on the boat when ...
... you wake up with a start to water dripping on your face. Upon closer inspection you find the vent window has closed and fat humongous stalactite raindrops are preparing to spatter all over your naked face and person.

... before getting out of bed and dodging raindrops you hear a tearing sound and realize you forgot to put the bag of kitty food inside the cabinet.

... Bill tries climbing out of bed and those raindrops find his bare back.

... when you step out of bed on to the cold floor and find it is also a cold, *wet* floor. Because during the night the wind has changed directions and is now blowing rain in thru the door.

... you go to do your morning 'business' and find on your list of things to do yesterday was dump the porta-potty.

... the public facilities doors are locked later than usual.

... you arrive at the dump station and there is a sign that reads "Closed for the Winter".

... in haste to do your morning 'business', you fail to notice the location of the porta-potty to the ledge it sits on and both you and it topple over.

... turning on the tea pot the flame sputters and dies because the propane tank is empty.

... trying to change the empty propane tank you find the bolt is too tight to undue.

... after getting in the shower and just wet, you realize you forgot to turn the water pump on.

... after getting out of the shower, dripping, and turn the pump on, then get all soaped up, the pump stops.

... after getting the pump to keep working and are ready to rinse soap and shampoo, the water quits, only this time because you forgot to check and see if the water tanks were full.

... the only day you think no one will stroll to your far end of the dock while getting out of the shower, they do.

... filling the water tanks and you don't pay attention to the exact second they become full and get another shower.

... making the bed you knock yourself out on the windshield wiper motor.

... pulling the sheets tight to make the bed, you notice that tale-tell sign of water line. On closer inspection you find the wind change in the night also leaked water under the pad you sleep on and all the sheet edges are wet.

... tidying the foot of the bed you find Bill has kicked the sack out from under the leak in the ceiling and the sheets are wet.

... carrying a load of garbage, laundry and mail you step on seagull do-do and slip on the dock, losing the grip on your load.

... the mail you were carrying flies out of your hand from a wind gust and you can't find a net.

... the load you carry is cumbersome and heavy, and it's a minus tide.

... you didn't notice it was an extra high tide and walk into the fish weighing pulley.

... arriving at the laundry and there are no washers available.

... putting the dollar bill in the machine at the laundry, there are no attendants and it keeps getting spit back at you.

... while waiting for the sheets to dry you begin working on the computer. After getting a full file in, hit the save button and the screen goes blank because you forgot to plug it in the night before.

... you see other boaters tying water hoses down to poles because of rumored winds.

... other boaters bring you buoys because of rumored winds.

... looking up at the Forest Service flag, it suddenly becomes board straight from the wind and now it's high tide.

... those rumored winds arrive and waves crash over the bow.

... tightening the bow lines a wave takes you in the face.

... you look out your metal laden boat and all of that salt water surrounding you and thunder suddenly crashes.

... doing dishes and a wind gust slams the boat, causing you to jostle the dish drainer perched on the rail, tipping it and its contents onto the floor, (smashing your favorite mug!).

... another boat comes screaming into the basin and you can't catch your coffee mug in time (smashing a favorite mug!).

...Bill isn't due home for two hours; you look in the icebox capable of holding two days groceries and find it's day three and the grocery store is already closed.

... Bill gets home early.

... enjoying the company of your husband while living on the far end of the dock, and another boat comes home.

... watching TV in a storm, you get seasick.

... you take the boat out fishing, the cats get seasick.

... a kitty that looks just like yours is cruising around on another boat.

... Bill pours himself into his twenty-plus year-old diving suit and a seagull laughs.

... immediately after washing the boat the seagulls begin target practice

... trying to sleep in a motel quiet-still bed, you can't.

... there is a klunk in the night and you remember that log floating in the basin.

... trying to take the boat out of the water and it's a minus tide.

... you get home later than expected, realize the dock is sheet ice, your arms are full, you have the wrong shoes on, and it's a minus tide.

... the radio phone rings and you find out there is a Tsunami warning in effect.

... out of kindness you allow another boat to raft, and they like to leave for fishing at four in the morning.

... the halibut (head) you were given was stolen by a seal or otter!

-—"Deck the Boat with Boughs of Holly,
Folly, Folly, La,
La, Lots of Folly!"

Epilogue

O ne day the year before, while we still lived in the motorhome in the driveway of the heavy equipment yard, Bill came home with a small box filled with little 2"x 4"x 4" blocks. When he got down on his hands and knees in the narrow walkway of the motorhome, I worried he'd sniffed too much jet fuel fumes.

"What are you doing?" I asked. Looking up, he said, "Building a boat," as he carefully laid out another block.

When he was done and sat back contemplating his work, I eyed the three-block wide, eight-block long rectangle, and said skeptically, "I don't see it."

Looking up, he seemed surprised and said, "it's a pontoon boat." Then added, "made of steel." I may not be the swiftest boat in the harbor, but even I know *steel doesn't float* and expressed my dismay.

He went on to explain, he could weld steel plates together 2' wide by 3' high, 32' long, making a pontoon and hold them together with two 6" pipes. Then build an 8' by 20' plywood box complete with toilet, tub, RV appliances, and full-size bed to sit atop the pontoons.

Although I voiced my opinion, when we got back Outside from living on the Bayliner, that winter he began collecting all the bits and pieces, and packed them in a 20' cargo container (something we call a connex box) we shipped north that spring.

When we got back to the Island, Bill asked the local shipyard owner if he could build a boat there and use his equipment. Henry, who looked like the Gorton Fisherman, asked Bill his plan. Bill told him he would weld the plates together into a rectangle 4' long, then pull the finished block out and away from the container, then weld the next pieces in place until 32' was extracted from the container. Henry scratched his head and said because he wanted to see how it could be done, yes, he could have the cargo container delivered to the yard and use his equipment.

For the next month all of Bill's spare time was spent at Henry's yard. Lots of fellows came to check out the project offering their suggestions, expressing their doubt, and scratching their own heads.

Finally launch day was at hand. Henry was amazed and told Bill he hadn't believed it could be done until he saw it come together. But the pontoon framework still had to get placed in the water and prove steel could float.

A fair crowd gathered on land and in North Cove on the boat docks across from the launch to see the spectacle. Bill had built a plywood platform on the pontoons and mounted a 60-horsepower Evinrude engine on the back. They slid the giant slings around the pontoons and ran the travel lift out over the water. The tide was high so it didn't have very far to be lowered into the harbor. You could almost hear a collective ooh as the straps went slack and "*The Barge*," what we'd begun to call the vessel, floated.

Ever the supportive wife, I climbed down the ladder and then perched on the plywood as Bill got the engine running. Soon Captain and First Mate were cruising out of the harbor heading around the spit for South Cove where we'd dock *The Barge*.

Ultimately, Bill would quit the helicopter job and we'd move to Prince of Wales year-round, until 2001 when we'd move Outside to Nevada and enter a different realm of aviation. And remember the dog Socks? We'd end up inheriting him and he'd grace our lives for another eight years. Our grandson Justin sure rocked our world, but tragically would only pass through. Those however are all stories for another time.

Adventures of the F/V KOLH

I

The time away from Craig had not been all fun and games. While Colby loved Sitka and the people he numbered among his friends, there was a certain unexplainable draw to that dreary town on Prince of Wales. After two months, he was looking forward to getting home.

Looking out over the churning sea under a sick gray sky, Colby wondered how rough the trip would be. He knew he should have left the last break in weather. Knowing it had been too soon, besides that was nearly two weeks ago, and he wanted to hit the cucumber opening near Chichagof Island before returning to Craig. Now he had to hurry. Untying the mooring lines, Colby swung the fishing vessel 'KOLH' away from the dock. With a worried frown seaward he headed north, rather than the preferred southern direction. With this wind he knew he would be hard pressed to make it in time tomorrow for the opening.

As Colby left the relative safety of the harbor, the wind began to immediately harass the little vessel. Standing with one foot inside the doorway and the other firmly planted on the deck, sometimes he felt like Popeye as he maneuvered his little twenty-six-foot homemade boat along the sea lanes. Continually scanning the horizon for floating debris and half sunk logs, Colby likened the hazards to Brutus continually trying to thwart Popeye's way.

As he caught movement from the corner of his eye, he saw a particularly nasty log occasionally bobbing above the surface. Its many broken branch ends ripping thru the water like a sharks fin could easily damage the fiberglass hull. Looking around him, Colby could see where storms of the past few months had littered the ocean with floating dangers.

Putting his mind back to the present problem, Colby climbed down into the little area he had divided off in the hull for his quarters. At five eleven,

Colby could hardly stand inside the cramped area. Easily reaching across the entire boat he picked up the chart he'd left on the little outcropping he called a table. Last night he remembered finding a passage that could trim several hours off his run time to Chichagof, if he was lucky.

Climbing back up the two steps to deck, Colby again scanned the area. Seeing nothing that could cause immediate harm his inner eye began to see the beauty. As always this trip was a salve to his troubled soul.

Despite the ugly gray day, there was a dignity to the rain battered islands. Or perhaps it talked to him when he looked at the trees trying not to sway to the onslaught of the wind. He mused he could almost hear them say, "There is pain, but it is ours, and we will endure."

Shaking himself a little, Colby again looked around, then checked his chart. Seeing the opening between two small islands off port, he hoped when he turned westerly the passage inside would be a little calmer.

Glancing at the instruments Colby could see the oil pressure was a little low. The previous day he had stocked up on oil, but hoped to come across a village that might keep his stores from being depleted. The wind and putta, putta, putta of the engine teamed efforts to stop all other sound, forcing Colby to keep company with himself. He was so used to doing this, he didn't even notice the internal and often external dialogue he kept.

Presently Colby was discussing the merits of the hot tub costume he'd seen at the Halloween Ball he'd attended in Sitka. Altho he argued that the guy who came as a dog with an owie, complete with bowl collar, was well worth mentioning. A quick glance at the instruments, slightly raised horizon and water ahead, and Colby resumed his ruminations. The winning costume had been two cute girls dressed as Siamese Martians. He didn't stop the deep throated laugh, and said aloud, "Now there would be a planet I could spend some time exploring."

The inside passage was calmer than he hoped and thought, 'If this keeps,' then said, "I'll make it on time," and finished in his mind, "to Chichagof." Another scan of instruments, horizon and immediate waterway, and Colby noted he'd have to add oil within a half hour.

Checking the charts he was startled to see a little village that should be coming up soon. Last night he hadn't noticed it. Angrily he thought 'how stupid!' Aloud he said, "That's just the kind of mistake that can cost you

Haard!", addressing himself caustically by his last name. Altho patient with others, he was much too hard on himself.

Colby Haard never thought of himself as Colby. All his life he had had to live with that silly name and the continual harassment of being called a Cheese Head that came with it. Anytime his father introduced him he always added the disclaimer, "We were honoring our Wisconsin ancestors that year."

Another look at the chart and then at the surrounding islands and Colby was reasonably sure he should see signs of the village very soon. The wind and rain had eased, lifting visibility to over a mile, but since the time change it would be dark within the hour. He hoped to be back underway and in a more open channel before then.

Seeing a break in the shoreline off to his right, Colby knew this was the inlet he was looking for. Easing starboard he saw a single light soft in the gloom. Slowing *KOLH*, he eyed shore.

Despite the heavy storms the water was still fairly clear down about three feet. He could see the bottom was covered with sand and a few small pebbles, not the usual jagged rocks of Southeast beaches. Gently he edged *KOLH* in as close as she would go. Throwing the anchor, he grabbed his 30.06 and went overboard. Luckily Colby's perception was good and he didn't go in more than knee-deep. He was ashore before the piercing cold touched his skin.

The path towards the light was well worn. Despite the red and yellowed leaves Colby recognized the blueberry and huckleberry bushes along the way. A low chuckle escaped when he thought of his first summer in Southeast.

As a child his family hadn't spent any time outdoors. Where he came from the biggest plant was usually grown indoors, and natural came from health food stores. So when he'd first arrived in Alaska, Colby had taken to the outdoors as a dog starved for water. When the early blueberries had ripened he had certainly indulged. Another chuckle escaped as he remembered how much he'd wished for certain facilities on the boat.

An unwelcome cough brought him abruptly back to the present. Without a feeling of fear, but with every single sense of his being alert and ready, his grip on the 30.06 tightened. Standing there, just looking at him, was the biggest, brown bear Colby had ever seen in his life, not that he personally went for walks with bears on a regular basis. This bear had to weigh over a thousand pounds. And it was between him and the safety of the village.

Suddenly the 30.06 didn't feel like a very big gun in view of this monster. A quick review of the information Colby had read and he knew if he shot it couldn't be a head shot as the bullet could bounce off the thick skull. All material emphasized a chest or shoulder shot and discouragingly said several bullets were usually necessary.

Very calmly Colby told the bear he really needed to get by. That he was only going to be here for a short time and that he had to get up to the store and then be on his way. Very politely he asked Mr. Bear if he wouldn't please move aside. The bear eyed him and lifted his muzzle sniffing Colby's direction. He knew the bear was thinking over his, Colby's fate, and had the irrational desire to argue his case.

Before he even had time to move, the bear disappeared in the thick bushes. Not sure if a sigh of relief was appropriate yet, Colby carefully hurried up the path, casting surreptitious glances over his shoulder.

When he emerged into a clearing a little building sat squarely in front of him. A crudely lettered sign leaned beside the door, as if it were a joke, proclaiming "Ye Ole Trading Post." Off to his left was another building, but much smaller. Colby figured it was a storage shed of some sort. Looking around he saw no evidence there was anyone here or had been here for the past fifty years.

Without much hope, Colby pushed at the door and was surprised when it opened into a well-lit, warm and even cozy room. He saw that the windows had been lined with aluminum foil, so no light showed thru.

The store portion was divided from a living area by a low counter slightly off center. Behind the counter lining the wall on shelves was a variety of canned goods, a few battered books, matches, and other small items. The living area had a neatly made cot in the corner, old wooden cook stove in the center of the wall, and counter with a wash basin and tidily arranged assortment of dishes.

Sitting at an old wood slab table on a chair carved from a stump was the wildest looking old man Colby had ever seen. At once he wasn't sure being here was a very good idea.

"Oh! Excuse me, I didn't mean to barge in on you like this, I thought this was a store and maybe you were open." Colby exclaimed a little abashed.

The old man scratched his ear, then tugged at a wild shock of white hair. Tilting his head towards Colby he bellowed, "What's that you say? Can't hear you! Dang ya, if yur gonna talk then speak up!!" Colby didn't quite know what to say as the old man reached for a gnarly old walking stick leaning next to him

A little concerned, he involuntarily stepped back when the old man pushed away from the table. Colby was glad the old guy didn't seem to notice his hesitancy. He watched as gnarled hands grabbed a glass off the counter, slammed it on the table, filling it with vodka from a bottle Colby hadn't noticed sitting beside the table, and shoved it towards him.

"Well don't just stand there, sit down!" The old man thumped his way back to the chair and dropped into it, grabbing up his own glass and downed the full contents. Colby felt like he'd stumbled into a twilight zone, but obliged and drank some of the vodka. As it burned its way down his belly he wondered how he was going to get out of here.

The old man refilled Colby's glass, tho it wasn't down an inch, and poured his own full. Thinking he'd better make a hasty retreat he shouted again at the fellow, "I'm sorry, I thought this was a store."

With an abrupt gesture the old man grabbed his walking stick, stomped to the counter and reached into a bowl. Colby was even more amazed as the old man put a hearing aid in his ear then said, "Hate these damn things! But they shore come in handy. Greyson's the name, Alex Greyson.", then stuck out his hand to shake. Colby felt a little off balance as he stood and wondered if it was the vodka or the environment, then shook the old man's hand.

"Sit down, sit down, it's been a spell since I've seen a body. The only company I get these days is that old bruin, Bore. Didn't happen to see a big brown ..." Colby didn't mean to interrupt but this was too weird, "Yea, yes I did. He was huge! Doesn't he bother you?"

"Bore? Naw, he just noses round. He's three years old now, been round here since he was a cub. Didn't never expect him to get so big, he was such a little feller. So what brings you round these parts?"

The swift change in conversation immediately brought Colby back to the reality of his situation. Thinking this would be a great place to come back and spend some time, the old guy was a real character, but he needed to be on his way.

"Oh. I thought this was a store," Colby explained once again, "and I could use some oil for my boat. I have enough, but if I could buy some, it would keep me a little more comfortable. Was this a store?"

The old guys ragged features softened a bit, "Yea, 'bout sixty years ago I put up this trading post. Used to be a village of Tlingit a few miles up the coast. But things change."

Watching as the old man drifted away in thought, Colby imagined it as it may have been before traditions changed and things were really wild and woolly. Though sometimes they could get that way, even now, he thought ironically.

Colby came back to present when the old man shoved away from the table. "What kinda oil? Got some stuff in the shed." Reaching for a big flashlight Greyson headed out the door.

The shed was neatly shelved and organized. Colby figured the old man didn't have much else to do with his time. Going to a back corner there were several cases of oil stacked there. He could see that there were also several gallon cases of vodka as well as an interesting assortment of parts and tools.

Knowing he couldn't have missed a boat, Colby looked closer and found they were aircraft parts. "You have a plane?"

Not a nosy person by nature he didn't mean to blurt out the question, but this whole place seemed to have put him a little off kilter. Greyson kept digging around, but answered over his shoulder, "Yea, a little Luscombe, It's over yonder a ways. Got a short little strip up back. This cove ain't always as friendly as it was today. It's on floats, but I got wheels too.

"Damn feds, took my medical 'bout ten years back. Said a man my age didn't have any business up in these skies. Way I figure it, I been around a helluva lot longer than that little snippet that listened to my heart! The skies I fly ain't so populated that anyone's in danger but me and the way I got it figured if the good Lord says it's my turn, don't make no never mind where I am. Aah! Here it is. Ya didn't say what kind ya wanted, Aeroshell 40 okay?" Colby would have preferred a 10W-30 weight with the approaching winter, but figured he'd have enough time to mix the two before something severe hit. "Yea, sure. That'd be great. How much do I owe you?"

For an uncomfortable amount of time Greyson studied Colby in the dim light. He wasn't sure what the old man was thinking and wondered if he was trying to figure out how much he could pay.

"You're the first person I seen in a long time. Not many folk come this way since they opened up that passage east a here. I'm a man who likes company," then added with a low laugh, "and vodka. You bring me back equal this much vodka and we'll call it even." Colby eyed the stack of boxes and wondered how long it would last the old man.

"You got yourself a deal, Mr. Greyson." A distasteful look crossed the old man's face, "Mr.! Hrmph," he said, "Mr. was my pappy! Greyson, that's just fine. You come back to see me when you got time." Colby vaguely wondered how the old guy had known he was in a hurry, but thanked him and started lugging the heavy box back to the *KOLH*.

Halfway down the path he wondered where 'Bore' was and if he could drop the box and grab his gun off the sling on his shoulder in time, should he need to. This thought was immediately followed by the question of whether Greyson would shoot him, if he killed the bear.

II

Altho it was only four thirty, it was already dark by the time Colby got back on *KOLH* and underway. Adjusting the instruments' night light down a bit allowed him to retain most of his night vision.

Though Colby didn't like the early darkness, too much room for introspection, he had never minded running in the dark. But he knew he'd have to keep his eyes open for obstacles as the way was fraught with hazards.

Settling his old leather jacket more comfortably around his shoulders, Colby shone the spot light about the waters ahead. Then checked the divers watch his mom had given him for Christmas the first year he came to Alaska. He figured if the wind stayed calm he would pull into Chichagof around midnight. "Good", he said, then finished in thought 'that will give me enough time to get some sleep and ready my gear before eight'.

While Colby had been with Greyson the storm had for the time being, blown itself out. The sky wasn't clear but there was a hole now and again that showed pale stars in the dark sky. 'If it wouldn't turn so blasted cold', Colby mused, 'a clear sky and the northern lights would be dancing.' Then he remembered it was only five and not likely they'd be out so early.

Another scan of instruments and horizon left Colby satisfied he could recheck the tide and charts. This new passage wasn't familiar and he didn't like exploring in the dark.

The tide book showed it would be low about nine fifteen. "Hmmm," he said, "a slight minus". The charts indicated the passage was shallow with a small channel that would be just enough for him to slide thru. He cursed as he realized in his haste to be underway he'd not done a thorough plan. Tiredly running his hand over his slightly weathered face he added checking the tide to his growing list of 'Things To Do Before Each Fishery.'

A slight bump brought Colby abruptly back to the present. A quick spot with the light and he saw that a small log had nudged the side of *KOLH*. Searching ahead he couldn't see any others, but then he was limited to a view of only about thirty-five feet.

A never-ending check of instruments and water let him know that the tide had dropped considerably since he'd left. A little uneasy he again checked the tide book and found there was still two more hours before low tide.

Standing in the doorway of the little vessel always made Colby consider his position in life. He hadn't been a fisherman more than a few years, and he'd certainly never intended to be one. Coming from where he did, a fish was brought home by dusty little boys from a muddy slough. Grown men, his mind recoiled at the emphasis on grown, held important jobs, again emphasizing, this time the word important.

Not wanting to remember the scenes that brought him here, Colby's mind turned to his departure. Before he became lost in thought a slight brightening in the sky caught his eye and he saw the remains of a falling star as it blazed thru a patch of cloudless sky.

At these times he sometimes felt insignificant. While he believed in something, "How else explain the sheer magnitude of this universe," he wondered aloud, he just wasn't sure what. Immediately he heard his sister's voice when she'd expressed horror in his views. Not that his sister was a Bible thumper, but she had strong ideas about God and how people fit into the scheme of things. His experiences had to make him wonder about such a God.

It had taken a long while, but finally he and his folks were able to talk, without continually 'going back'. His father had never said anything against Colby's new life. His mother had said she couldn't understand *why*. But they both had let him know that they loved him and would accept anything he chose to do. Colby chuckled and raised a bushy blond eyebrow as he said "Did they have any choice?"

'Choices,' his mind began and his voice finished, "now there's a thought." What-Ifs began to play havoc with his heart:

What-IF he'd taken sweet Megan O'Reilly to the senior prom rather than, his mind paused and he said, "Colorful." Then in an aside he thought 'colorful is a nice word'. Without knowing it he nodded his head in agreement with himself. "But sleazy is more accurate." he started, then finished aloud, "Rather than Carol Hansen." A deep laugh rumbled as he remembered *that* night.

Then a sobering What-IF jumped in to ruin the image as Sara Jenkins flew in on her broom.

What-*IF* he'd spent more time with the bio-chemist instead of that pig headed Professor.

What-*IF* he'd talked to Chief Butler, rather than First Class Davis.

What-*IF* he'd ..., the shrill of the depth finder shattered these thoughts, flinging Colby back to the perils of navigation in Southeast waters.

A flash of the spotlight showed no debris, but the foreboding presence of jagged rocks. A quick glance at his watch showed he'd spent far too much time with those of his family and those he didn't necessarily love. Sending unpleasant thoughts to the unloved ones, he checked the charts and reset the sounder on the depth finder to three fathoms.

The chart showed the next several miles were covered with rocks and shallows. Tide wouldn't be completely low for another forty-five minutes. Colby shouted to the trees looming ominously on either side of him to relieve some tension. The hoarse screeching of a blue heron as it flew off in a huff, gave him immense satisfaction.

Shining the spotlight around, Colby saw a pair of eyes reflecting back at him. Not the bright red of a carnivore but the glowing green of an herbivore convinced him it was probably one of the little Sitka deer that inhabited these islands. A paradise for hunter, survivalist, and enviro-terrorist alike, the islands abounded with deer, bear, and wolves.

The instruments showed that the oil was again getting low. Reluctant to leave his vigil on rock patrol Colby figured he could wait a little while longer before adding more. The beginnings of the depth finders sound had Colby frantically looking for signs of danger.

Slowing *KOLH* even further he was barely inching thru the cold black waters. Shining the light overboard and straight down he was dismayed to see the rock-strewn bottom of the strait just below him.

A grating thunk plunged Colby's stomach to his toes as *KOLH* came to an abrupt stop, ramming him into the little doorway and upsetting his balance. Cutting power completely, he set the engine to idle, then hurried round the door to peer into the clear waters.

Looking down, it became painfully obvious that *KOLH* was lodged in a crevice on the edge of the only rock large enough to stop it. Disgusted at the turn of events he wondered if he could reverse off, as the tide was still going out and he could become really stuck if he didn't get away immediately.

Easing the throttle in and pulling on reverse didn't seem to work. Vaguely, Colby wondered if he could go overboard and push *KOLH* off, but dismissed the notion right away. Diving alone was bad enough, but to do so at night under an unstable boat was pushing the limit. Grateful he hadn't smashed the prop he wondered if the hull had been damaged.

Knowing the easiest way to find out, Colby descended thru the little doorway into his living quarters. Checking the floor for signs of water he was relieved to see dry plywood. Kneeling on the foot of his bed along the starboard wall he ran his hand down the bow line but didn't feel any moisture. Squatting under the table, he picked up the hot plate that must have fallen off in the crash and put it back. Feeling along the port seam, again he was grateful for no signs of wetness.

Going back atop he descended into the fish box in the stern. Shining the light around Colby couldn't see any sign of damage, but felt around all the edges anyway. Knowing the boat was only hung up by the bow he hadn't expected to find anything wrong.

Extremely annoyed, Colby checked the tide book once again. Altho by now he knew exactly what time low was. Realizing there wasn't anything he could do but wait for the incoming tide, he began a check of the engine. "Well," he said, 'now is a perfect time to add oil.' Switching on the little generator, he figured he might as well heat a tin of stew and sleep for a few hours until he could get off that "blasted rock," he muttered aloud.

III

Setting the alarm for midnight Colby felt he was probably being a bit optimistic. Altho the tide would be half way in by then he didn't think it would clear *KOLH* before early morning. Thinking he was too wired to sleep he lay there sorting thru the past twenty-four hours.

The clang of the old-fashioned windup clock brought Colby to with a start. Naturally a light sleeper, combined with the fact he *had* to be alert most all the time, usually gave him the advantage of an internal clock. For a brief moment he was disoriented, but reality flooded in on him within seconds.

Hastily he threw on his heavy jacket. The missing buoyancy in his step let Colby know the vessel was still stuck. Turning the flashlight into the waters he could see *KOLH* was still lodged but it wouldn't be long before she floated free and clear. Disappointed but not surprised, he reset the alarm for another few hours. This time he didn't hesitate to sleep.

A gentle rocking before the alarm went off let Colby know the tide had released its tenacious hold on *KOLH*. Still several hours out, he grumbled at the fact he couldn't run at more than a few knots until out of the shallow passage. Daylight wouldn't be for many more hours so he kept the spotlight in constant motion, trained on the waters ahead, beside, and sometimes even under him.

Knowing that with the incoming tide he didn't need to worry about the passage, he set the depth finder for two fathoms anyway. With a grim expression he noted on the chart the idiosyncrasies of the passage, as he now knew them.

The narrow finally came to an end. Altho it was still dark, judging by the chart and where the instruments told Colby he was, he got the sense he'd been dumped into a large strait. It had been a while since he'd passed thru this area so the feel of his exact location wasn't really clear. The putta, putta, putta of the engine increased in tempo and Colby felt a tremendous weight lift off his shoulders as he began to run at a fair speed.

Either during the night or Colby had simply outrun it, the main body of the storm was south of him. Still slightly overcast, the sky had a hint of color around the mountain edges rising out of the deep water off to his right. The clear white feel of the salt morning and the fuzzy pink of the beginning day gave a texture to the air that he hoped to capture in water paint if he had a few minutes.

Despite the long night Colby didn't feel all that tired. A new fishery always brought challenge and each one held its own excitement and unpredictable adventure. With an eye on the water, the instruments, and now the clock, Colby made a mad dash for Chichagof.

A movement port caught his eye and he smiled as a little pod of Dall's porpoise began escorting him north. Looking like a miniature version of an Orca, so grossly named Killer Whale, many of the tourists, and skippers he had to admit, who passed thru these waters each year mistook them for baby Orcas. Their antics always brought a smile to his lips. With a jaunty tilt and a self-impressed air he was ready for whatever challenges Brutus threw his way.

Checking the chart, Colby found the passage to the little cove he had decided to dive in. A glance at his watch and he groaned when he discovered it was already eight-thirty. "Timed seasons! What a cocky idea!" he groused as he threw the anchor and began assembling his diving gear.

While a tall fellow, the past few years of his own cooking had slimmed him down and he had to add five pounds of lead to his belt. Checking the air tanks for the umpteenth time he was satisfied they were full. A quick glance around encouraged him that he was alone in this particular area and should be able to harvest the thousand-pound limit within the seven-hour fishery.

A last look at the boat assured Colby he hadn't forgotten anything on the 'Anchoring To Do List.' Slipping overboard into the cold clear waters always gave him a thrill. A sudden chuckle almost unsettled his mask when he realized maybe it wasn't a thrill, but a chill as the icy waters tried to penetrate his wet suit.

The world below was just that, another world. The inhabitants here didn't worry about clocks, bells, or whistles. It was a silent world, one that Colby was comfortable in.

Looking along the rocky bottom he never tired of the beautifully colored, frilled sea anemones, dark green chitons, scurrying crabs, or feathery little tube worms. The seemingly suspended clear jelly fish made him pause and the sundial starfish, some as big as platters and with at least forty arms, never ceased to amaze him. Despite the abundant population of sea life, he became concerned when he hadn't spotted any of the dark purple, red, or orange sea cucumbers.

The horribly ugly, horny ooze was known locally as 'poor man's abalone', and overseas considered a delicacy.

Colby thought about the first time he'd dived for the squishy football shaped things and wondered how on earth anyone could bring themselves to eat such a disgusting blob. Once on land, he'd sliced into one, surprised to find little fingers of delicate white meat which turned out to be quite appetizing. He was very glad seafood was healthy.

When another half hour of searching proved nearly futile, Colby surfaced, knowing his tanks were low on air anyway. Realizing he was running out of time; he figured he'd go further north to another cove he had in mind.

Hastily pulling the anchor he set a course for northwest. Mentally calculating how much time it would take to get there, get set, etc., he became furious with Fish and Game for setting such ridiculous times. The new engine he wanted to put in *KOLH* would take almost all his meager reserves and he'd counted on the cucumber fishery to see him thru the winter. 'At this rate,' he thought unhappily, 'I'll be starved by Ground Hogs Day!'

The cove Colby had chosen wasn't as private as he liked, so settled for the deeper waters of the narrows.

Again anchoring and donning gear, over the side he went. When his feet didn't touch bottom, he realized he'd stepped into a swift current. Grabbing the first rock that went by he nearly shook hands with the open claw of a disturbed crab. While still trying to right himself he was delighted to see cucumbers everywhere

With his feet under him, Colby tried to stand but was immediately pushed over backwards. Ruefully, knowing how a turtle feels on its back, awkwardly he righted himself, clinging to the nearest rock. 'This is not going well,' he thought to himself, subconsciously knowing when not to speak aloud.

Looking the area over, Colby could see where the current had washed a small ravine among the rocks and even a small strip of the white bright of a sandy bottom.

Knowing cucumbers couldn't find anything to eat there it was easy to dismiss that as a place to pick. To the walls of the rock to his right clung about fifty cucumbers but the stream of seaweed showed the current was even stronger.

Littered across the ocean floor to his left were a hundred or more, but the current wasn't steady, whipping the eel grass back and forth. The thought of 'choices' jumped into his head. A sudden laugh disturbed his mask, causing him to start as the icy water hit his face.

Crawling across the ocean floor Colby's sense of humor knew he looked a sight and was glad he was alone. His feet were all but useless, giving him ballast more than anything else. As one hand grabbed a cucumber and tried to stuff it in the wandering bag at his side, the other grasped the nearest rock he could get hold of. In trying to put the errant glob in the sack the current usually pushed him off balance and he'd have to right himself, find another rock to anchor with and start again. A slow drawn-out process, the morning passed too quickly.

Immerging only long enough to stow the cucumbers and change air tanks, Colby had collected almost a full fish box when the tiny beep of the alarm warned him he had fifteen minutes before season closure.

Surveying the rocks close at hand, he saw three cucumbers within easy reach. Another check of his watch and was shocked to find he had less than ten minutes to be on board.

Altho he hadn't been alone in the area; Colby hadn't noticed any Fish and Game and was relieved. Having started from the boat and worked away from it, he snorted, giving in to *bizimungu* and realized it could take at least ten minutes to get back to *KOLH* and out of the water. Abruptly turning back he almost collided with a Dall's porpoise that was gliding up to see what he was doing.

Colby wasn't sure, but thought the change in tide had increased the current. Using both hands to hold himself and still needing a third to move on, his traitorous internal clock began the final count down.

Three minutes and he was still a hundred feet from the boat. A dark shadow moving in off from his right sent a slight chill down his spine. Altho he didn't like to dive with Orcas, 'Killer Whale does carry a rather ominous sound' he thought, for once he hoped that was what it was.

Fifty-feet and two minutes, and Colby began to feel a slight vibration. The shadow was growling. Wishes of whales were crushed, but ever the optimist he hoped it was only another diver coming to see how he'd done.

At the same time Colby came up under *KOLH*, the shadow of the other boat came to a stop and the harsh beep on the second alarm announced to the water world that he was late. Shoving the heavy bag over the side, another pair of hands helped lift it off him. The weak sun managed to cast a beam that glared in his eye off the shiny badge of the uniformed man standing above him.

Feeling like a scene out of an old grade B movie, the brown clad game warden leaned down and growled "You're *late*, son!" Having the good sense not to laugh, Colby wanted to turn round on himself to see if when he wasn't looking someone had tacked a sign to his back that said "kick me".

Knowing that catching violators was this guy's job, briefly Colby wondered if he would understand about the bear, then the rock and now the current. Figuring he wouldn't, and not wanting to whine aloud, he nodded his head in agreement.

Handing him the little five by seven award for his efforts, the warden left with a tip of his hand. Colby didn't even bother to look at it, just tossed it in the box with the rest of his 'important' papers, and changed into dry clothes.

The cloud cover was complete, blocking out what bit of daylight remained. Seeing that the cucumbers were secure, Colby settled down for the evening. After fixing a bite to eat, again he mused over the events of the past few days. Remembering the touch of the morning, he dug out the box of watercolors and began to paint.

Having plenty of time for a second picture, with a nasty glint in his eye Colby painted in an ominous brown shadow that promptly got eaten by a bigger, black and white shadow.

IV

A stronger beat to the maritime rock-n-roll woke Colby from a satisfying dream of brown uniformed men dancing to the castanet clatter of cranky crabs. A slight smile played under his bushy mustache as he lay there planning his day.

It was a few miles south where the fish processor would be set up and then he could begin the trek "home", he murmured aloud.

How comfortable that word lay on his mind. Then a laugh as he realized "technically, I *am* home.", he said, then amended the statement with a thought, 'but if I get the hankering for pizza it's tough to get delivery service here!'

With that thought Colby jumped out of bed. Poking his head out the door he could see the clouds had moved back in and a cold sharp blast of wind hit him in the face. Rummaging in the box he kept his few clothes; he dug out an old woolen pair of pants. A thick underlayer of black silk, 'you rake you' he thought, and he was set for the day.

Within the hour Colby had sold the cucumbers to the processor and was making his way south. A scan of the horizon showed there hadn't been an improvement in the log situation, 'and it's only going to get' "worse" from here', he alternated between thinking and speaking aloud.

He'd fiddled with the engine a little last night and she seemed to be running a bit smoother. A constant check of the oil gauge and he was pleased to see it hadn't perceptibly dropped as usual.

By early afternoon his run time thru the straits and narrows had brought him into Goddard Hot Springs and a fine soaking mist. Altho Colby hadn't planned his route specifically to come this way, a sudden shiver made up his mind to stop and visit friends at the hot springs.

Idling up to the little rickety dock Colby tied the mooring lines off and secured the door. Pulling the Helli-Hansen rain coat closer he began his way up the path.

Some worn out leaning stairs topped him out into a wide flat area. The buildings off to his right were in good repair, but he was dismayed to see that the public buildings to the hot springs had been torn down and lay in ruin.

Hurrying thru the rain he headed into the stand of trees that rimmed the area. Finding the path that led to his friends' house, he picked his way over roots and around stumps.

Every time he came here he wondered why they didn't make a decent path. Then remembering the little rough cut yellow cedar cabin, the tall scruffy Michael and very earthy Jane, he wondered why he'd wondered.

A low growl brought Colby back to the darkened forest. A twinge went thru him as he knew he didn't have his gun. Freezing, he looked round with his eyes only, a black spot off to his left catching his attention.

Turning ever so slowly towards it, he barely had time to cover his face as the black beast landed squarely on his chest knocking him down, and the wind out of him.

In the time a man has to blink an eye, Colby had horrible visions of the different bear attacks he had read about. Being alone so much he had plenty of time to read. In as much as another blink, and with the help of a severe tongue washing, Colby knew he'd been attacked by Kolh, the huge husky of Michael and Jane. Grabbing a handful of hair behind his ears he pulled the heavy dog off him. Kolh stood there wagging his tail all over his furry body.

About that time Colby heard footsteps and Michael shouted several suggestions to the dog. In the familiar fluid movement, so amazing in such a big man, Michael pulled him to his feet, clapped him on the shoulder, and began leading him to the cabin. The entire event had taken less than thirty seconds and left Colby a little dazed.

"Yo! Did you just get here?" Michael asked in his rumble, "Jane will be real happy to see you. She just finished up some rhubarb wine and needs a guinea pig. Me, I can't stand the stuff. I'm still trying to get that barley to make something. Where you been? How long you here for? Where you headed?"

In Colby's mind he pictured stopping and turning to Michael with hands on hips and asking him with exasperation, 'how can a man of your stature, carry on so? It seems more fit for a woman!' But never the antagonist or thinking of himself as a chauvinist, he smiled and let Michael go on. Jane met them halfway. Those wild colored skirts and jangling bangles the only obvious quirk from the past of the quiet woman.

"Colby, how good to see you." she said as she tucked one arm in his. "Has Michael talked an ear off already? Kolh didn't hurt you did he?"

"No, no, I'm fine." Colby smiled as he looked down at the dog trying to get between all of them. He had found the scared pup in a log jam, a little wild but so starved it overcame his natural fear. Knowing the little dog would grow too big for the boat, Colby thought Michael and Jane's would be a perfect place for him.

That night lounging in the hot springs and over too many huckleberry daiquiris they tried to come up with a name for the mess of fur curled by the fire.

Colby had been telling them stories of his childhood and about visiting his gruff old grandfather Lloyd, at his farm. The old goat was beyond rich but ornery by heaps. He'd made a peculiar clause in his will about certain things the family had to do, to 'earn' their inheritance. When he'd helped Colby with the boat he thought it a grand joke it was named KOLH. Keep Old Lloyd Happy.

Michael gawffed and said that was *his* middle name and by golly that little dung heap was going to earn his keep. Kolh didn't seem to mind and had proved his worth over time.

Entering the little cabin Colby couldn't help marvel, as he always did, that in 1994 one could enter a room that was pure 1800s and it be real.

Michael had built the cabin years ago when he and Jane had first moved to Southeast straight out of Berkeley. Altho it had running hot and cold water it wasn't from the traditional water faucets, but two pipes out of the wall with on/off valves. They were lucky to have the hot water from the springs.

The kerosene lamps were placed about with care, and plentiful, which enhanced the cabins feeling of warmth. The homemade table was covered with a bright yellow cloth and a vase of Labrador tea sprigs sat in the center. The willow furniture was a concession from natural Southeast, but blended beautifully, and Jane had made bright pillows and cushions for color and comfort. Altho Colby could see himself in the "yuppie" lifestyle, when visiting here, sometimes he wondered.

"Are you hungry Colby?" Jane asked. "We were going to have a lite supper and then go into the springs. We've herring roe on kelp with rice, some fiddleheads, and oysters." Colby couldn't help laughing aloud. A little indignant Jane demanded "What's so funny?"

"I love to visit here because it's so comfortable. And train of thought brought me to my family and friends back home. Do you have any idea what that menu sounds like to Outsiders?" Using the term Alaskans have for those from the Lower 48.

A thoughtful look crossed Jane's features and then she smirked, "That's why they're there and we're here." An exaggerated wink from Michael and the tone was set for the evening.

Much later that night, completely relaxed for the first time in days, Colby lay thinking about his life. It certainly hadn't turned out the way he'd planned, and he wasn't doing what he wanted, but for the moment, he was happy.

A week passed quickly and one morning Colby woke to the most glorious, sunshine-filled day he'd seen in over a month. The wind was calm and the sun tried to warm the early November hours. It was time to continue south.

Waving off to Michael and Jane, the putta, putta, putta of the engine carried him out of the little harbor. The seas were smooth and the wind was out of the north. 'Good', he thought, "I'll be home early."

The Dall's porpoise escorted him for over an hour and a spectacular display by a couple of humpback whales carried him thru another.

Before he knew it, he was passing into Klawock inlet. He could see the cliffs ahead and Fish Egg Island loomed starboard with Sunnahae off port.

Pulling into White Pass for fuel, John shouted "it's been awhile, what've you been doing?"

Thinking a minute, Colby played the past few weeks back in his mind, the huge thousand plus pound bear, hanging up on the rock, the current while diving and *friend*, (his mind had a hard time thinking of the Coast Guard as *friends*, although they could be useful he conceded), and the week at the hot springs. Instead he said, "Not much. Been up around Sitka."

As he pulled around the spit Craig sat on and into South Cove, Colby saw the few changes that had occurred since he'd been gone.

John and Carol's boat was wrapped tight as a Christmas present so obviously they were off to Tennessee. Dan had a blue tarp over his little morphydite he called a boat so it must have been nasty here too. There was a different boat in the end slot and *ROTORWASH* was gone, but he didn't think they'd pulled out yet, they weren't due to leave before mid-November.

Sam and his dog Patty were climbing on *PEPE*. The *AURORA* and *STARLITE* were in but the *DANDY LION* and *PRINCESS* were gone. He saw the old guys off the *L.X.* and *REIGN'ERE* talking and Bob, with his rolling gait, was taking that old mangy poodle Salt out for a stroll.

As he tucked in his spot behind the piling at the end of the pier and looked out over Cemetery Island and up Port St. Nicholas, he thought, 'It's good to be', then paused looking around again, and said aloud, "home."

Also by J. Butler Kyle

US 395 Series
No Exit Necessary: Reno, NV to Adelanto, CA
No Exit Necessary: Reno, NV to Adelanto, CA

Standalone
Tales From The Dockside

Watch for more at https://jbutlerkyle.com/.

About the Author

J. Butler Kyle has thousands and thousands of hours traveling America's roads with her husband as they crisscrossed the US. All the way pouring over maps and reading aloud the local history and flavor of the country they were seeing, researching things to see and do along the route.

They have lived in over one hundred places in the US, including an island in the Gulf of Alaska. Twenty-four years were in some form of an RV. All those locations were aviation related, including aerial firefighting while J. was Crew Chief on a Single Engine Air Tanker (SEAT).

J. has written other travel and visitor guides (Prince of Wales Island, Alaska); humorous short stories for *Aviation USA* and *RV Life*; expanded the Southeast Alaska portion of *The Milepost*; and ghost-written three memoirs. Her first self-published book, *Tales From the Dockside*, is a collection of fun and often embarrassing vignettes of her and her husband's two years living on a boat in the Gulf of Alaska.

Northern Nevada is where J. calls home with said husband, their family of kitties, and whatever strays wander in. She loves to garden, capture photographs, and of course travel. J. once helped evacuate a casino of all its cash, but that's another story.

You can reach J. at jbutlerkyle@yahoo.com, visit her website at jbutlerkyle.com, or find her on Facebook at J. Butler Kyle, Scribe.

Read more at https://jbutlerkyle.com/.